DEFENDING THE SANCTITY OF MARRIAGE

JOSEPH FIELDING MCCONKIE

BEN HAVEN BOOKS

Published and printed in the United States by
Ben Haven Books

ISBN: 978-0-9895792-1-6

Library of Congress Control Number

For other works from this author, including:

50 Truths The Devil Doesn't Want You To Know

Valiant in the Testimony of Christ

Between the Lines

In electronic and paperback form, please visit:
www.McConkieBooks.com

For bulk purchases or general questions, please email:
info@McConkieBooks.com

Contents

Preface

If we truly believe that "marriage is ordained of God" and that it was intended to be "for time and for all eternity," we must also believe that it is a sacred union and that it can be built and strengthened only with sacred principles. A marriage performed at the altar of the temple is a marriage consecrated to God. Scripture records thousands of years of testimony that the altar is both the place of sacrifice and the place of covenant. It is a perfect symbol to attest that all the blessings of the gospel exist because of the atoning sacrifice of Christ. In and through his Atonement all the truths of salvation are preserved and all covenants sanctified.

In the *Dictionary of Word Origins* we are told that "To *sacrifice* was, originally, not to give up, but to make something holy." The word comes from the Latin *sacre,* meaning holy, plus *facere,* which means to make. Thus it carries the meaning of a sacred oath. (Joseph T. Shipley, *Dictionary of Word Origins,* New York, NY: Philosophical Library, 1945, p. 308) The purpose of this brief work is to enhance the readers' understanding of the sanctity of the "sacred oath" or covenant of marriage. It is of particular interest to this work that the word sanctity (or sanctify) was intended to give description of something that was ordained as sacred or inviolable. The Latin *sanctus,* from which the word sanctify comes, is the source of the English word *saint.* (John Ayto, *Word Origins,* London, UK: A & C Black, 2008, p. 435) Surely there is a special responsibility that comes with bearing the name Latter-day Saint.

It is to Latter-day Saints that I write and it is from the perspective of the restored gospel that the meaning of scriptural texts that existed before the Restoration is unfolded. It is not a new religion that we claim but rather the faith and understanding of the ancients as they restored their faith to us. The missionaries sent from the heavens to teach Joseph Smith included Adam, Moses who penned Adam's history, an Elias from Abraham's day (perhaps Abraham himself), and Elijah who restored the sealing power. Thus our doctrines are their doctrines and our faith their faith.

It is through their eyes that we see the story of Eden as both singular to Adam and universal to all humankind. It is through that which they restored to us that we see the marriage of Adam to Eve as the divine pattern and the key that unlocks the meaning and purpose of all else that followed as the gospel was taught to our first parents. From the Book of Moses we read: "The Gospel began to be preached, from the beginning, being declared by holy angels sent forth from the presence of God, and by his own voice, and by the gift of the Holy Ghost. And thus all things were confirmed unto Adam, by a holy ordinance, and the Gospel preached, and a decree sent forth, that it should be in the world, until the end thereof; and thus it was. Amen." (Moses 5:58-59) The "holy ordinance" to which reference is made was the law of sacrifice. Thus the ordinance of sacrifice, which is a type for the Atonement, confirms the efficacy of all other ordinances with the crowning ordinance being marriage.

So it is that the story of Adam and Eve becomes our story, for the doctrines of salvation are everlastingly the same and there is but one path that leads back to our divine parents. Sister Julie Beck stated the matter thus: "The Creation of the earth was the creation of an earth where a family could live. It was a creation of a man and a woman who were the two essential halves of a family. It was not about a creation of a man and a woman who happened to have a family. It was intentional all along that Adam and Eve form an eternal family. It was part of the plan that these two be sealed and form an eternal family unit. That was the plan of happiness." (*Teaching the Doctrine of the Family,* Aug. 4, 2009, www.lds.org/pa/rs/pdf/CES_2009_Beck_eng.pdf, p. 2)

This work includes a consideration of selected gospel principles such as the fatherhood of God and the doctrine of agency, and the principle that no unclean thing can enter into the presence of God. The question could be asked as to what such principles have to do with the sanctity of marriage? The response is that all correct principles find their most perfect expression in the sacred union of the man and woman. I have chosen to comment on principles that are commonly misunderstood or the strength of which has been lost to us by our failure to teach them. It is in such principles, correctly understood, that we find a defense against the sophistry of the world and the hope-diminishing ignorance of some of our own number.

We cannot build the house of our understanding out of faulty notions and expect it to be a sanctuary from the world. Illustrations are legion. Those who use scriptural arguments to sustain that which is unholy have missed the purpose of holy writ. Of his scriptures the Lord has said, "there is no unrighteousness in them." (Doctrine and Covenants 67:9) "Wherefore teach it unto your children, that all men, everywhere, must repent, or they can in nowise inherit the kingdom of God, for no unclean thing can dwell there, or dwell in his presence; for in the language of Adam, Man of Holiness is his name, and the name of his Only Begotten is the Son of Man, even Jesus Christ, a righteous Judge, who shall come in the meridian of time." (Moses 6:57) To argue that God's love for all his children supplants the teachings of this or any divine law argues against the law and the wisdom of the God who gave it. Indeed, it is to change God for there is no dispensation of the gospel in which the decree has not gone forth that no unclean thing can enter his presence. In like manner, parents who suppose that the doctrine of agency allows their children to act without consequence should they choose to do so have built the house of their understanding on the sand. Such a course will not produce the same results as teaching children that agency is the power to act righteously.

All good doctrine leads to the temple and its covenants. It is "in the ordinances of the temple," stated President Howard W.

Hunter, that "the foundations of the eternal family are sealed in place. The Church has the responsibility—and the authority—to preserve and protect the family as the foundation of society." ("A Temple-Motivated People," *Ensign,* February 1995, p. 2)

Chapter 1

In the Image of God

Marriage was ordained of God for the blessing and salvation of his children. That there might be no question as to its nature and purpose God himself performed earth's first marriage uniting the man Adam and the woman Eve as "one flesh" in a union that was to be as eternal as God himself. It was in that sacred ceremony that the command was given that they multiply and replenish the earth. "[A]nd all this," the scripture declares, "that the earth might answer the end of its creation." (Doctrine and Covenants 49:16)

Save it be for this sacred union of the man and the woman both the purpose of their creation and their salvation remain incomplete. They were created to be part of each other, each giving life and meaning to the other. "[N]either is the man without the woman, neither the woman without the man, in the Lord." (1 Corinthians 11:11) When the Creator joined Adam and Eve together, as the progenitors of the human race, we do not learn that he set any limit to the continuance of their marriage relationship. The phrase, so often used in marriage ceremonies, "until death do ye part," finds no place in holy writ or the plan of God. Everything in the entire plan of salvation assumes that there will be life after death and that the united family is to continue throughout the eternities. One could not imagine the ordinance of baptism, or any other gospel ordinance for that matter, containing the words "until death do ye part." Revelation declares that "all covenants, contracts, bonds, obligations, oaths, vows, performances, connections, associations, or expectations, that are not made and entered into and sealed by the Holy Spirit of promise, of him who is anointed, both as well for time and for all eternity" are to be of "no efficacy, virtue, or force in and after the resurrection from the dead." (Doctrine and Covenants 132:7)

In the book *A Compendium of the Doctrines of the Gospel*, a respected expression of the doctrines of the Restoration, written by Elder Franklin D. Richards of the Quorum of the Twelve, aided by Elder James A. Little, the authors explain the doctrine here involved thus:

"Man, in his fullness, is a twofold organization—male and female. Either being incapable of filling the measure of their creation alone, as it requires the union of the two to complete man in the image of God, for in Gen. 1:27, it expressly says, that he was created male and female in the image of God. Therefore, without the proper union of the sexes, man would be less than what God created him.

"There is a comprehensive significance in, 'The Lord God said, it is not good that man should be alone.' (Gen. 2:18) It speaks of no particular period of man's life, and has no limit in its application. The entire narrative of the union of Adam and Eve, in the second chapter of Genesis, intimates the designed inseparable relationship between man and wife, in marriage as ordained of God." (Franklin D. Richards and James A. Little, *A Compendium of the Doctrines of the Gospel*, Salt Lake City, UT: Deseret Book Company, 1925, pp. 117-118)

The Most Ancient and Most Modern of All Gospel Stories

The crown jewel of the creation story as told by Moses in the Book of Genesis is that of Adam and Eve. The earth we are told was given to them, they were to have dominion over it. The first commandment given them was to "multiply and replenish [more correctly *fill*] the earth with their seed. This covenant with all its attendant blessings was thus to be granted to their children who were to walk in their paths that the earth might fill the purpose of its creation for such is the work and glory of God, "to bring to pass the immortality and eternal life of man." (Moses 1:39) "If it were not so, the whole earth would be utterly wasted at his [Christ's] coming." (Doctrine and Covenants 2:3)

Let us recount the events of Eden, which our readers who have been through the temple will recognize as a veiled temple story. The main characters in our story are God, our Eternal Father; the man Adam; and the woman Eve. As is so often the case in such stories the names of its characters are chosen with purpose and become an important part of the instruction being given. The name Adam comes from the Hebrew *ad'-um* which carries two distinct meanings. The first being a human being or mankind, the second being the name of our father Adam. How the word *ad'-um* is rendered in the text is purely the translator's choice. It may well be that no two translations of this story are or have been rendered the same. From the Book of Abraham we learn that the name Adam means "first father." (Abraham 1:3) Thus the use of the name Adam makes the story both personal and universal. This is confirmed in Moses 1:34 wherein the Lord says, "And the first man of all men have I called Adam, which is many."

God invites Adam to give his wife a name which he does with the Spirit of inspiration: "And Adam called his wife's name Eve, because she was the mother of all living." The text then adds, "for thus have I, the Lord God, called the first of all women, which are many." (Moses 4:26) Thus the name Eve like the name Adam carries a universal meaning. All women in marriages ordained of God assume the name Eve as their husbands assume the name Adam. It is the oldest story ever told and the story with which the family history of all who have been married in the temple begins.

The story begins in the first chapter of Genesis in this language: "And God said, Let us make man in our image, and after our likeness: and let them have dominion over the fish of the sea, and over the fowl of the air, and over the cattle, and over all the earth, and over every creeping thing that creepeth upon the earth.

"So God created man in his *own* image, in the image of God created he him; male and female created he them." (Genesis 1:26-27) Of necessity we must ask and answer well the question as to whom God is speaking when he says, "Let us make man in our image, after our likeness." The generally accepted answer in the world of Jewish and Christian scholars is that God is conversing with lesser deities who constitute heaven's governing council. The answer accords harmoniously with Abraham's account of the creation where the text reads thus:

"And the Gods took counsel among themselves and said: Let us go down and form man in our image, after our likeness; and we will give them dominion over the fish of the sea, and over the fowl of the air, and over the cattle, and over all the earth, and over every creeping thing that creepeth upon the earth.

"So the Gods went down to organize man in their own image, in the image of the Gods to form they him, male and female to form they them." (Abraham 4:26-27)

These Gods so spoken of do indeed form the heavenly council and are identified earlier in the text as the noble and great among the host of God's children who are yet to inhabit the earth. (Abraham 3:21-22) They are referred to by President Joseph F. Smith in his vision of the redemption of the dead as "choice spirits" who even before they were born "received their first lessons in the world of spirits and were prepared to come forth in the due time of the Lord to labor in his vineyard for the salvation of the souls of men." (Doctrine and Covenants 138:53-56) According to this revelation they included "our glorious Mother Eve, with many of her faithful daughters." (Doctrine and Covenants 138:39) Thus the principle is set that all who live upon this earth lived before and are of the family of God. The Psalmist describing this same scene said, "God standeth in the congregation of the mighty; he judgeth among the gods." He concludes his thought with a reminder to us all, "Ye *are* gods; and all of you *are* children of the most High." (Psalms 82:1, 6) As spirits we were fathered by the "most High" in heavenly realms long before we were born in to this mortal sphere. "The Family: A Proclamation to the World" states the matter thus:

"All human beings—male and female—are created in the image of God. Each is a beloved spirit son or daughter of heavenly parents, and, as such, each has a divine nature and destiny. Gender is an essential characteristic of individual premortal, mortal, and eternal identity and purpose." (Paragraph 2) (The First Presidency and Council of the Twelve Apostles of the Church of Jesus Christ of Latter-day Saints, "The Family: A Proclamation to the World," September 23, 1995; *Ensign*, November 1995) James E. Talmage described the matter thus:

"We affirm as reasonable, scriptural, and true, the eternity of sex among the children of God. The distinction between male and female is no condition peculiar to the relatively brief period of mortal life. It was an essential characteristic of our pre-existent condition, even as it shall continue after death, in both disembodied and resurrected states. … [The] scriptures attest a state of existence preceding mortality, in which the spirit children of God lived, doubtless with distinguishing characteristics, including the distinction of sex, 'before they were created naturally upon the face of the earth.'" ("The Eternity of Sex," *Young Woman's Journal*, October 1914, p. 602)

Let us have the matter plain: Adam and Eve had both father and mother. The initial command to "leave father and mother" and to cleave unto each other was first given to them and subsequently to us. (Moses 3:24) They could hardly have left parents they did not have. "Have ye not read," Christ asked of the Pharisees who came to tempt him, "that he which made *them* at the beginning made them male and female, And said, For this cause shall a man leave father and mother, and shall cleave to his wife: and they twain shall be one flesh?" (Matthew 19:4-5)

The declaration that Adam, and we will add Eve, were created from the dust of the earth is a metaphor intended to remind us that their divine parents partook of the elements of this earth before Adam and Eve were conceived. (Moses 6:58-59) In other words, all physical things were created out of physical element. On this matter Joseph Fielding Smith observed that "The *Book of Mormon,* the *Bible,* the *Doctrine and Covenants,* and the *Pearl of Great Price* all declare that Adam's body was created from the dust of the ground, that is, from the dust of *this ground, this earth.* Moreover the Lord said to Adam, that if he partook of the fruit of the tree of the knowledge of good and evil, he should surely die. 'By the sweat of thy face shalt thou eat bread, until thou shalt *return* unto the ground—for thou shalt surely die—for out of *it* [i.e., *the ground*] wast thou taken: for *dust thou wast,* and unto dust shalt thou return.' Now how could he return to the dust of the earth, if his body was not taken from it?" (*Doctrines of Salvation: Sermons and Writings of Joseph Fielding Smith,* compiled by Bruce R. McConkie, *Vol. 1,* Salt Lake City, UT: Bookcraft, 1954, pp. 1:90-91)

As Adam was created from the dust of the earth so was Eve and so were you and so was I. Enoch quoting from the writings of Adam preserves this communication between Adam and God for us: "That by reason of transgression cometh the fall, which fall bringeth death, and inasmuch as ye [all mankind] were born into the world by water, and blood, and the spirit, which I have made, and *so became of dust a living soul,* even so ye must be born again into the kingdom of heaven, of water, and of the Spirit, and be cleansed by blood, even the blood of mine Only Begotten; that ye might be sanctified from all sin, and enjoy the words of eternal life in this world, and eternal life in the world to come, even immortal glory." (Moses 6:59, italics added)

The account of Eve's birth is most beautiful, particularly so in a day when there is so much confusion about the role of women. Symbolically, she was not taken from the bones of Adam's head nor from the bones of his heel, for it is not the place of woman to be either above the man or beneath him. Her place is at his side, and so she is taken, in the figurative sense, from his rib—the bone that girds the side and rests closest to the heart. Thus we find Adam declaring: "This I know now is bone of my bones, and flesh of my flesh; she shall be called Woman, because she was taken out of man." (Moses 3:23) Eve, unlike the rest of God's creations, was of Adam's bone and of his flesh, meaning that she was equal to him in powers, faculties, and rights.

The official statement of the First Presidency, "The Origin of Man," states: "It is held by some that Adam was not the first man upon this earth and that the original human being was a development from lower orders of the animal creation. These, however, are the theories of men. The word of the Lord declared that Adam was 'the first man of all men' (Moses 1:34), and we are therefore in duty bound to regard him as the primal parent of our race. ...

"The Church of Jesus Christ of Latter-day Saints, basing its belief on divine revelation, ancient and modern, proclaims man to be the direct and lineal offspring of Deity. ... [God] formed every plant that grows and every animal that breathes, each after its own kind, spiritually and temporally—'that which is spiritual being in the likeness of that which is temporal, and that which is temporal in the likeness of that which is spiritual.' He made the tadpole and the ape, the lion and the elephant, but He did not make them in His own image, nor endow them with godlike reason and intelligence. Nevertheless, the whole animal creation will be perfected and perpetuated in the Hereafter, each class in its 'distinct order or sphere,' and will enjoy 'eternal felicity.' That fact has been made plain in this dispensation (see D&C 77:3)."

I have learned over the years that people see in this document what they are prepared to see but I do not know how our language could allow for a more expressive and enlightening statement than the declaration that man is the *"direct and lineal offspring of Deity."* (First Presidency of the Church of Jesus Christ of Latter-day Saints, "The Origin of Man," *Improvement Era,* November 1909, pp. 75-81 [notation standardized]; italics added)

In the Book of Moses, Enoch traces his genealogy from his father back to Adam, of whom he says, "...Adam, who was the son of God, with whom God, himself, conversed." (Moses 6:22) In like manner, Abraham speaking of the patriarchal order attested that "It was conferred upon me from the fathers; it came down from the fathers, from the beginning of time, yea, even from the beginning, or before the foundation of the earth, down to the present time, even *the right of the firstborn,* or the first man, who is Adam, or first father, through the fathers unto me." (Abraham 1:3; italics added) The honest truth seeker must take seriously these declarations that Adam was the "son of God," even the "firstborn." The reader may ask: does this not contradict the doctrine that Jesus is God's Only Begotten Son? It does not. Christ was the only son begotten of God in the "flesh" meaning the only child of the Father who was born of a mortal mother and thus had blood coursing in his veins. The blood was Mary's gift to her son because of it he could lay down his body and die. From his Father he inherited the capacity to take it up again and live. God could not give his son what he did not have and God does not have the capacity to die but Mary could do so.

The Bible Dictionary explains the matter in this way: "Before the fall, Adam and Eve had physical bodies but no blood. There was no sin, no death, and no children among any of the earthly creations. With the eating of the 'forbidden fruit,' Adam and Eve became mortal, sin entered, blood formed in their bodies, and death became a part of life. Adam became the 'first flesh' upon the earth (Moses 3:7), meaning that he and Eve were the first to become mortal. After Adam fell, the whole creation fell and became mortal. Adam's fall brought both physical and spiritual death into the world upon all mankind (Helaman 14:16-17)." (Bible Dictionary, "Fall of Adam," p. 670) None have taught this principle with greater plainness than father Lehi who said, "And now, behold, if Adam had not transgressed he would not have fallen, but he would have remained in the garden of Eden. And all things which were created must have remained in the same state in which they were after they were created; and they must have remained forever, and had no end. And they would have had no children; wherefore they would have remained in a state of innocence, having no joy, for they knew no misery; doing no good, for they knew no sin. But behold, all things have been done in the wisdom of him who knoweth all things. Adam fell that men might be; and men are, that they might have joy." (2 Nephi 2:22-25)

So it was that Satan who "knew not the mind of God" came to entice the Woman to partake of the tree of the knowledge of good and evil and showing that he too can quote scripture told her "then your eyes shall be opened, and ye shall be as gods, knowing good and evil." (Genesis 3:5) When Adam joined his wife in the partaking of this fruit we read that "they sewed fig leaves together, and made themselves aprons." (Genesis 3:7) The apron was not made of palm leaves, or of the maple, or of an apple tree but of the fig tree for it is the symbol of fertility and was used to modestly cover that part of the body that we associate with the power of procreation which they had now obtained. Covered with leaves they now represented the tree of life which symbolized the purpose of their creation and the blessings promised to them of endless seed. It is in this union and this union only that Adam and Eve assume the image and likeness of God and become one with him as they have been commanded to become with each other.

Before God allowed our first parents to leave Eden they were clothed in "coats of skins," (Genesis 3:21) which we can only suppose were that of lambs, to stand as a constant reminder to them that in and through the blood of the lamb they would find protection for all the effects of the fall and eventually reward them with the fullness of all gospel blessings. Through their obedience to this ordinance taught them in Eden this understanding was given them by an angel of the Lord:

"And after many days an angel of the Lord appeared unto Adam, saying: Why dost thou offer sacrifices unto the Lord? And Adam said unto him: I know not, save the Lord commanded me. And then the angel spake, saying: This thing is a similitude of the sacrifice of the Only Begotten of the Father, which is full of grace and truth. Wherefore, thou shalt do all that thou doest in the name of the Son, and thou shalt repent and call upon God in the name of the Son forevermore. And in that day the Holy Ghost fell upon Adam, which beareth record of the Father and the Son, saying: I am the Only Begotten of the Father from the beginning, henceforth and forever, that as thou hast fallen thou mayest be redeemed, and all mankind, even as many as will. And in that day Adam blessed God and was filled, and began to prophesy concerning all the families of the earth, saying: Blessed be the name of God, for because of my transgression my eyes are opened, and in this life I shall have joy, and again in the flesh I shall see God. And Eve, his wife, heard all these things and was glad, saying: Were it not for our transgression we never should have had seed, and never should have known good and evil, and the joy of our redemption, and the eternal life which God giveth unto all the obedient. And Adam and Eve blessed the name of God, and they made all things known unto their sons and their daughters." (Moses 5:6-12)

Teaching Their Children the Divine Plan

Adam and Eve recorded these things in a book of remembrance, "for it was given unto as many as called upon God to write by the spirit of inspiration; And by them their children were taught to read and write, having a language, which was pure and undefiled." They were instructed that this was to be the order of things from the "beginning" to the "end of the world." The divine plan has not changed. And "a genealogy was kept of the children of God. And this was the book of the generations of Adam, saying: In the day that God created man, in the likeness of God made he him; In the image of his own body [not a divine essence but a body as real as that which you and I have], male and female, created he them, and blessed them, and called their name Adam...." (Moses 6:5-9)

The text says these were the "children of God," and sheds its greatest light on the eternal nature of the family if we simply allow it to mean what it says: we are indeed God's children. Brigham Young said, "Adam was as conversant with his Father who placed him upon this earth as we are conversant with our earthly parents. The Father frequently came to visit his son Adam, and talked and walked with him; and the children of Adam were more or less acquainted with the Grandfather, and their children were more or less acquainted with the Great Grandfather; and the things that pertain to God and to heaven were as familiar among mankind, in the first ages of their existence on earth as these mountains are to our mountain boys, as our gardens are to our wives and children, or as the road to the Western Ocean is to the experienced traveler." (George Q. Cannon, editor, *Journal of Discourses, Vol. 9*, Liverpool, UK: Cannon, p.148)

Such is the foundational story upon which all gospel truths rest. It is the background for teaching the three pillars of eternity—the Creation, the Fall and the Atonement. All that follows in the book of Genesis, and all other scriptural records, is rooted in the story of the creation and marriage of the man Adam to the woman Eve. To miss this is to miss the true purpose and meaning of all other gospel principles. They are but the fruits produced by the tree of life which Adam and Eve became in their sacred union. To change the story is to change our understanding of who we are and why we were created. It is to change the work and glory of God; indeed, to change the God we worship. Standing at the heart of the story is the divine utterance that the man and the woman are his offspring having been created in his image and likeness. In the full and proper sense we obtain the image and likeness of God in the same manner that Adam and Eve did and that was in the sacred union of marriage.

It is my story and your story. It is a universal story acted out again and again when a son of God takes one of God's daughters to Eden represented by the house of the Lord and is married in his name and by his power for time and all eternity. In this ceremony they like our first parents obtain the promise of eternal life and the power of procreation throughout the endless expanses of eternity thus enabling the earth to answer the ends of its creation and God's sons and daughters to do the same.

Chapter 2

The Promises Made to the Fathers

The promises of God come by covenant and are intended for the blessing and exaltation of all his children. This is the reason covenantal ordinances must be performed by the proper authority and administered with exactness. The baptismal prayer, the sacramental prayer, and all the ordinances of the temple are expected to be administered in the exact and precise language in which they were revealed. They are not to vary from one individual to another. This is our assurance that the blessings flowing there from are to be the same for all who enter into them. One person cannot be preferred above another; both the man and the woman are to be treated with perfect equality. The realization of the blessings of the covenant are based on personal righteousness and can be obtained in no other way.

All gospel covenants were first known to father Adam and mother Eve. As originally administered they were expected to pass as life itself to their children through the endless generations. The Book of Moses tells us that the "same Priesthood, which was in the beginning, shall be in the end of the world also." (Moses 5:7) If the priesthood is the same then the ordinances with their attendant promises must be the same also.

In our day many have chosen to modify or change the nature of these covenants. It is a day in which people feel it their right to argue with or counsel God. After the Aaronic Priesthood had been restored with the authority to baptize a number of people immediately sought to be baptized. When the Church was organized on April 6, 1830, they were required to be rebaptized. Some of their number questioned the necessity of their rebaptism. The Lord in response to Joseph Smith's inquiry in their behalf stated the principle, which applies to all gospel ordinances, in this manner: "Enter ye in at the gate, as I have commanded, and seek not to counsel your God." (Doctrine and Covenants 22:4) Salvation and its attendant ordinances cannot be bought or sold, nor is it open to negotiation, or modification of any kind. To change the ordinances or to modify the way they are performed is to change God. One would do as well to argue with the tide, to tell the falling rain that it was unjust and must change with the times, or to march in a parade of protest against the scorching sun.

Restoring the Promises Made to the Fathers

On the night of September 21, 1823, Moroni appeared to the still-youthful Joseph Smith and delivered to him what may well be the greatest discourse on the Old Testament ever given. This was to prepare him for the responsibility that would be his in translating the Book of Mormon and to evidence that this ancient record came in fulfillment of the vision of the Old Testament prophets. In most instances, Moroni rendered the Old Testament texts as we have them preserved for us in the King James Bible. One notable exception is the manner in which he rendered Malachi's prophecy about the return of Elijah and his turning the key so that the hearts of the fathers could in the full and proper sense turn to their children and the hearts of the children to their fathers. The words of Malachi are rendered in this manner, "Behold, I will send you Elijah the prophet before the coming of the great and dreadful day of the Lord: And he shall turn the heart of the fathers to the children, and the heart of the children to their fathers, lest I come and smite the earth with a curse." (Malachi 4:5-6)

Assuring us that this is a correct translation, the Savior quoted it in exactly the same language while giving his great covenant discourse to the Nephites. (3 Nephi 25:5-6) In expanding the text, Moroni was illustrating that the Spirit of revelation can always reach beyond the written word to bring additional light and truth. (Doctrine and Covenants 52:9; Alma 5:46-47)

> *"For behold, the day cometh that shall burn as an oven, and all the proud, yea, and all that do wickedly shall burn as stubble; for they that come shall burn them, saith the Lord of Hosts, that it shall leave them neither root nor branch.* And again, he quoted the fifth verse thus: *Behold, I will reveal unto you the Priesthood, by the hand of Elijah the prophet, before the coming of the great and dreadful day of the Lord.* He also quoted the next verse differently: *And he shall plant in the hearts of the children the promises made to the fathers, and the hearts of the children shall turn to their fathers. If it were not so, the whole earth would be utterly wasted at his coming."* (Joseph Smith-History 1:37-39)

As the text begins, God promises that in a not too far distant day he would "reveal the Priesthood by the hand of Elijah." That is, in and through the keys that Elijah restored we would gain an understanding by the Spirit of revelation of the purpose of the priesthood, its powers, authorities, and purposes that we could not otherwise have. Before this the priesthood would be restored. This would be the labor of Peter, James, and John; then Elijah could come and "reveal" its purpose. That purpose centers in the promises made to the fathers—Abraham, Isaac, and Jacob—and is to keep the earth from being "cursed" or as Moroni stated it, "utterly wasted." As we shall learn, the earth fills its destiny when the ordinances of salvation are performed with the crowning ordinance being the sealing of a man and woman together for time and eternity. One may ask, "Did they have all these ordinances including the ordinance of eternal marriage in Old Testament times?" To which our response is, "How could they restore to us authority they did not have?"

Again it is to the Book of Genesis (Genesis mean beginnings) to which we turn to tell our story. It begins with father Abram whose name in the old language means "exalted father." As a result of the covenant he and Sarah made when they were married for time and eternity he received a new name which was Abraham. The suffix "am" which is added to his name means "nations," or "peoples." Thus Abraham's new name is an expression of the covenant promises that were now his. The text reads thus: "Now the LORD had said unto Abram, Get thee out of thy country, and from thy kindred, and from thy father's house, unto a land that I will shew thee: And I will make of thee a great nation, and I will bless thee, and make thy name great; and thou shalt be a blessing: And I will bless them that bless thee, and curse him that curseth thee: and in thee shall all families of the earth be blessed." (Genesis 12:1-3)

Here Abram is promised that in and through him "all families of the earth" will be blessed. The text offers no explanation as to how this is to happen.

We get an expanded view of what is involved in Genesis 17, which reads as follows: "And when Abram was ninety years old and nine, the LORD appeared to Abram, and said unto him, I *am* the Almighty God; walk before me, and be thou perfect. And I will make my covenant between me and thee, and will multiply thee exceedingly. And Abram fell on his face: and God talked with him, saying, As for me, behold, my covenant *is* with thee, and thou shalt be a father of many nations. Neither shall thy name any more be called Abram, but thy name shall be Abraham; for a father of many nations have I made thee. And I will make thee exceeding fruitful, and I will make nations of thee, and kings shall come out of thee. And I will establish my covenant between me and thee and thy seed after thee in their generations for an everlasting covenant, to be a God unto thee, and to thy seed after thee. And I will give unto thee, and to thy seed after thee, the land wherein thou art a stranger, all the land of Canaan, for an everlasting possession; and I will be their God." (Genesis 17:1-8)

Here we learn that not only is Abram to become the father of many nations but that the covenant he made with the Lord was to extend out and embrace his children and his children's children throughout countless generations. Indeed, as we piece the story together we learn that his seed is to be as countless as the stars of the heaven or as all the dust upon the earth.

Of special interest is the idea that Abram in making this covenant is not just acting for himself but is obligating his unborn children to the terms of the covenant. Knowing the jealousy with which God guards the principle of agency this suggests that covenants were made long before birth into mortality and that we are born with an obligation to our fathers and mothers reaching back through the generations. No one is born without obligation to others. This is inherent in our having been born into the heavenly family of which we are all a part. This finds expression in an epistle written by Joseph Smith to the Church using as his illustration the recently revealed principle of baptism for the dead. Had the principle of eternal marriage been revealed at this time, we assume that ordinance would have been used as his illustration. The letter read:

> *"And now, my dearly beloved brethren and sisters, let me assure you that these are principles in relation to the dead and the living that cannot be lightly passed over, as pertaining to our salvation. For their salvation is necessary and essential to our salvation, as Paul says concerning the fathers—that they without us cannot be made perfect—neither can we without our dead be made perfect. And now, in relation to the baptism for the dead, I will give you another quotation of Paul, 1 Corinthians 15:29: Else what shall they do which are baptized for the dead, if the dead rise not at all? Why are they then baptized for the dead? And again, in connection with this quotation I will give you a quotation from one of the prophets, who had his eye fixed on the restoration of the priesthood, the glories to be revealed in the last days, and in an especial manner this most glorious of all*

subjects belonging to the everlasting gospel, namely, the baptism for the dead; for Malachi says, last chapter, verses 5th and 6th: Behold, I will send you Elijah the prophet before the coming of the great and dreadful day of the Lord: And he shall turn the heart of the fathers to the children, and the heart of the children to their fathers, lest I come and smite the earth with a curse. I might have rendered a plainer translation to this [that being Moroni's], but it is sufficiently plain to suit my purpose as it stands. It is sufficient to know, in this case, that the earth will be smitten with a curse unless there is a welding link of some kind or other between the fathers and the children, upon some subject or other—and behold what is that subject? It is the baptism for the dead. For we without them cannot be made perfect; neither can they without us be made perfect. Neither can they nor we be made perfect without those who have died in the gospel also; for it is necessary in the ushering in of the dispensation of the fullness of times, which dispensation is now beginning to usher in, that a whole and complete and perfect union, and welding together of dispensations, and keys, and powers, and glories should take place, and be revealed from the days of Adam even to the present time. And not only this, but those things which never have been revealed from the foundation of the world, but have been kept hid from the wise and prudent, shall be revealed unto babes and sucklings in this, the dispensation of the fullness of times." (Doctrine and Covenants 128:15-18)

The most perfect rendering of the Abrahamic covenant is found, naturally enough, in the Book of Abraham. It reads thus:

"My name is Jehovah, and I know the end from the beginning; therefore my hand shall be over thee. And I will make of thee a great nation, and I will bless thee above measure, and make thy name great among all

nations, and thou shalt be a blessing unto thy seed after thee, that in their hands they shall bear this ministry and Priesthood unto all nations; And I will bless them through thy name; for as many as receive this Gospel shall be called after thy name, and shall be accounted thy seed, and shall rise up and bless thee, as their father; And I will bless them that bless thee, and curse them that curse thee; and in thee (that is, in thy Priesthood) and in thy seed (that is, thy Priesthood), for I give unto thee a promise that this right shall continue in thee, and in thy seed after thee (that is to say, the literal seed, or the seed of the body) shall all the families of the earth be blessed, even with the blessings of the Gospel, which are the blessings of salvation, even of life eternal." (Abraham 2:8-11)

You Were Born to Bless Others

So once again we read that "all the families of the earth are to be blessed" by the "literal" seed of Abraham. It is his seed that is to hold the priesthood and to carry the message of salvation to the ends of the earth with all the attendant "blessings of salvation, even of life eternal." Eternal life is the key word in this passage. Eternal life is the name of the kind of life that God our Heavenly Father lives. Eternal life consists of two things. It consists of a continuation of the family unit in eternity and it consists of inheriting the power, dignity, honor, glory, might and omnipotence of the Father himself. That is called the fullness of the glory of the Father. So, when Joseph Smith said that God himself, finding he was in the midst of spirits and glory, ordained laws whereby they might advance and progress and become like him, he was talking about people gaining eternal life. (*Teachings of the Prophet Joseph Smith*, compiled by Joseph Fielding Smith, Salt Lake City, UT: Deseret Book, 1976, p. 354)

For our purposes let us think about eternal life as consisting of a continuation of the family unit in eternity. And that means celestial marriage. Celestial marriage opens the door to the continuation of the family unit in eternity. If the family unit continues in eternity then people have eternal increase. They have, in the Prophet's language, spirit children in the resurrection.

This is the promise given of God to Abraham for him and for his posterity. To get a better sense of what is involved let us return to the Book of Genesis. This story and these texts are given as patterns. The whole message of the book of Genesis is family, family, family. That is family past, family present, and family future.

We have read the Lord's promise as found in the Book of Abraham. Let us now read another one, a later one, as found in Genesis. It is clear that Abraham is deeply concerned relative to the promise he has received about his family. He does not have any children as yet, though the Lord has told him he will have posterity without end. So, he importunes the Lord and gets another revelation. "And the LORD said unto Abram, after that Lot was separated from him, Lift up now thine eyes, and look from the place where thou art northward, and southward, and eastward, and westward: For all the land which thou seest, to thee will I give it, and to thy seed for ever. And I will make thy seed as the dust of the earth: so that if a man can number the dust of the earth, *then* shall thy seed also be numbered. Arise, walk through the land in the length of it and in the breadth of it; for I will give it unto thee." (Genesis 13:14-17) Abraham's seed is going to have the land of Palestine in the resurrection.

Let us read yet another passage. He importunes the Lord again saying: "And Abram said, Lord GOD, what wilt thou give me, seeing I go childless, and the steward of my house *is* this Eliezer of Damascus? And Abram said, Behold, to me thou hast given no seed: and, lo, one born in my house is mine heir. And, behold, the word of the LORD *came* unto him, saying, This shall not be thine heir; but he that shall come forth out of thine own bowels shall be thine heir. And he brought him forth abroad, and said, Look now toward heaven, and tell the stars, if thou be able to number them: and he said unto him, So shall thy seed be. And he believed in the LORD; and he counted it to him for righteousness." (Genesis 15:2-6)

After that Sarah gave Hagar to Abraham as a wife, and she bore Ishmael, so he had seed in that sense. But, that was not to be the royal lineage and so three men visited Abraham. They are described as holy men. It seems perfectly clear to us that they were the First Presidency of the Church at that time. (Doctrine and Covenants 107:29) They visited Abraham to give him blessings and are the ones who said that his wife would have a child. It was on this occasion that Sarah laughed and was confused.

Abraham has the promise that he and his seed will have the gospel and all its blessings. Then Abraham was told that Sarah would conceive and that his seed would be in Isaac. Of Sarah the Lord said: "And I will bless her, and give thee a son also of her: yea, I will bless her, and she shall be *a mother* of nations; kings of people shall be of her." (Genesis 17:15-16) And also: "Sarah thy wife shall bear thee a son indeed; and thou shalt call his name Isaac: and I will establish my covenant with him for an everlasting covenant, *and* with his seed after him." (Genesis 17:19) The holy men to whom we made earlier reference told him the same thing and in due course Isaac was born.

Then something happened that, in many respects, is the most dramatic thing in the Old Testament. The Lord told Abraham to take Isaac up on Mount Moriah and sacrifice him. And Abraham believed God and knew that if he did that God would raise Isaac from the dead, so that in Isaac his seed would flourish according to the promise. The Book of Mormon tells us that the offering of Abraham on the Mount, his willingness to sacrifice his only Begotten Son, was in similitude of the sacrifice of God our Father and his only son on the cross when our Lord worked out the infinite and eternal atoning sacrifice. (Jacob 4:5)

Among faithful people in ancient Israel, through all the ages from Abraham's day onward, the favored illustration and the favored text to teach the people that the Only Begotten Son would be sacrificed to bring immortality to men, would be the willing obedience of Abraham and Isaac to do as the Lord had commanded.

At this point in Abraham's life, there on Mount Moriah, the angel of the Lord called unto Abraham out of heaven and said, "By myself have I sworn, said the Lord, for because thou hast done this thing, and has not withheld thy son, thine only *son* [his only son as far as the inheritance and promises are concerned]: That in blessing I will bless thee, and in multiplying I will multiply thy seed as the stars of the haven, and as the sand which is upon the sea shore; and thy seed shall possess the gate of his enemies. And in thy seed shall all the nations of the earth be blessed; because thou hast obeyed my voice." (Genesis 22:16-18)

It is significant to notice that in each instance the promise is given only to those who obey the voice of the Lord. To them the Lord promised they would be a blessing to all people. Now, that is quite graphic and that happens to be the way it reads in latter-day revelation. The *Jewish Study Bible* renders the text in a manner that is useful. It reads, "All the nations of the earth shall bless themselves by your descendants." (Berlin, Adele and Brettler, Marc Zvi, editors; Fishbane, Michael, consulting editor, *The Jewish Study Bible*, New York, NY: Oxford University Press, 2004, p. 47) The meaning of the two renditions is the same, but the *Jewish Bible* is more graphic. It crystallizes the thought in a better way. All the nations of the earth bless themselves if they believe and obey the gospel.

The Marriages of Isaac and Jacob

We need to add to our story the account of Abraham sending his trusted servant, Eliezer, back to his kindred to get a wife for Isaac. Before doing so Eliezer was required by Abraham to swear an oath by the God of heaven and earth that he would not take a wife for Isaac from among the Canaanites among whom they dwelt but that he was to go back to the country of Abraham's kindred. To Eliezer the promise was given that the angel of the Lord would go before him, and he would make the right choice. The promise found its fulfillment in his being led to find Rebekah. She was the daughter of Bethuel and the granddaughter of Nahor, Abraham's brother. This part of the family stayed behind in Padan-aram (northern Syria) when Abraham moved to the land of Canaan with his wife, Sarah, and his nephew, Lot.

Rebekah went one evening to fill her water jar at the well. As she was returning, a stranger in charge of a string of laden camels stopped this young woman who is described as "very fair to look upon" and asked for a drink. She gave it to him and offered to draw water for his camels as well. This was the sought-for sign to signify she was the girl that the Lord had chosen. Eliezer gave her a gold earring and two gold bracelets.

Abraham's servant then inquired who her parents were and whether there was room in her home for him to lodge that night. She courteously invited him to do so.

The servant disclosed his mission to her family and gave them gifts from Abraham. After some discussion and Rebekah giving her consent she traveled back to Canaan with Eliezer. Before doing so she was given a blessing in which she was told that she would be *the mother* of thousands of millions." (Genesis 24:60) That would mean billions of people. This blessing came by the power of the Spirit. It is speaking of the eternal increase that grows out of celestial marriage.

Isaac received the same blessing, the same promise, that had been given to Abraham. The Lord God appeared to Isaac and said: "And the LORD appeared unto him, and said, Go not down into Egypt; dwell in the land which I shall tell thee of: Sojourn in this land, and I will be with thee, and will bless thee; for unto thee, and unto thy seed, I will give all these countries, and I will perform the oath which I swear unto Abraham thy father; And I will make thy seed to multiply as the stars of heaven, and will give unto thy seed all these countries; and in thy seed shall all the nations of the earth be blessed; Because that Abraham obeyed my voice, and kept my charge, my commandments, my statutes, and my laws." (Genesis 26:2-5)

The Book of Genesis also contains a marvelous account that concerns Jacob and his marriage. This is about as good an illustration as we have of how a strong-minded, faithful woman can influence a righteous husband to do the proper thing. In this account Rebekah is running the family. She may well be the strongest character mentioned in the whole body of revealed writ. In the account Rebekah said to Isaac: "I am weary of my life because of the daughters of Heth: If Jacob take a wife of the daughters of Heth, such as these *which are* the daughters of the land, what good shall my life do me?" Esau, Jacob's twin, had just done that very thing. So Rebekah in effect is saying that if Jacob marries out of the Church as Esau has, if he takes to wife a daughter of the land, one of these nonmembers of the Church, what is her life worth? 'What is there left for me if my other son forsakes the gospel covenant and marries a nonmember of the Church?' In this way Rebekah stirred Jacob up, and Jacob did what he ought to have done on his own initiative. The account says: "And Isaac called Jacob, and blessed him, and charged him, and said unto him, Thou shalt not take a wife of the daughters of Canaan." That is to say: 'Thou shalt not marry out of the Church. My father, Abraham, said that in my seed and continuing in yours the blessings would come.' So, in this patriarchal blessing, as it were, Isaac says: "Arise, go to Padan-aram, to the house of Bethuel thy mother's father; and take thee a wife from thence from the daughters of Laban, thy mother's brother." The important thing here is that you marry the right person. "And God Almighty bless thee, and make thee fruitful, and multiply thee, that thou mayest be a multitude of people; And give thee the blessing of Abraham, to thee, and to thy seed with thee." (Genesis 27:46; 28:1-4)

Jacob went and did as his father commanded. He married Leah and he married Rachel. The Lord appeared to him, as he had appeared to Abraham and to Isaac, and he gave him the promises he made to his father and grandfather. In one account it says: "the LORD stood above" Jacob and said, "I am the LORD God of Abraham, thy father, and the God of Isaac: the land whereon thou liest, to thee will I give it, and to thy seed; And thy seed shall be as the dust of the earth." This is the promise that Abraham had. No one can have seed as the dust of the earth in this life. That is eternal increase. "And thou shalt spread abroad to the west, and to the east, and to the north, and to the south." And then, the Lord gives that great promise: "And in thee and in thy seed shall all the families of the earth be blessed." (Genesis 28:13-14)

Go and Do Thou Likewise

The story of Abraham, Isaac, and Jacob gives us a sense and feel of how things were done anciently. There are other similar Old Testament accounts. Genesis is a scripture that talks about families. Once the Lord has chosen his illustrations, and has given his patterns, and selected the prophets who were to exemplify to all men the principles, then he is in a position to say to all their descendants, 'Go and do thou likewise.'

Let us now see what has happened in modern times. There are two passages that are of particular importance. One of them is in Section 110 in the Doctrine and Covenants. This account tells us what happened on April 3, 1836. We are particularly concerned with the ministry of two people on that day. The account says: "After this [Moses returning to restore the keys of the gathering of Israel], Elias appeared, and committed the dispensation of the gospel of Abraham" to Joseph Smith and Oliver Cowdery, promising that in them and their seed all generations after them would be blessed. Did you hear it? God came to Abraham and to Isaac and to Jacob and he said to each of them in turn that in them and in their seed all generations should be blessed. And lo and behold, he says it to Joseph Smith in modern times; he says exactly what he said to Abraham, Isaac and Jacob. The grandeur and the wonder of it are almost beyond belief. Can you think of anything better? Joseph Smith is being told that he is going to get the kind of blessings that Abraham received. Then the account says that Elijah, the prophet who was taken to heaven, without tasting death, came down; and restored the sealing power. (Doctrine and Covenants 110:12-16)

One more passage is necessary for us to get the full picture of what is involved in this story. We find it in what the Lord told Joseph Smith about Abraham. It announces to us that "Abraham … hath entered unto his exaltation and sitteth upon his throne." Now, notice, "Abraham received promises concerning his seed, and of the fruit of his loins." These are the promises made to the fathers. Is it not a marvelous thing that God himself says to Abraham, to Isaac and to Jacob, and then to Joseph Smith, that in them and their seed all generations shall be blessed? This is the promise of eternal increase. We would ask then if there is anyone else to whom this promise has been given. By response we can say that the President of the Church has, like Joseph Smith, received this blessing. In addition to the President of the Church his counselors in the First Presidency and all the members of the Quorum of the Twelve have received this promise but it does not end there. The Lord does not give blessings to Abraham, Isaac and Jacob, and to the President of the Church, and the Quorum of the Twelve that are not available to every faithful elder and sister in the Church. It does not make one particle of difference what one's position is. All the blessings of heaven come on the basis of personal righteousness. Everyone who is married in the temple for time and all eternity has received exactly the same promise that God gave to Abraham, Isaac, and Jacob. It is part of the marriage ceremony. The same language is used in every marriage ceremony that is performed. Go back and listen to the ceremony that is performed in the sealing room at the altar. It speaks of promises given to Abraham, Isaac, and Jacob, of the promise that in us and in our seed blessings will accrue to unnumbered millions. Everyone who is married in the temple who keeps that covenant has the assurance that he will have eternal increase; that their posterity will be like the dust of the earth and the stars of heaven in number.

We return to the revelation: "Abraham received promises concerning his seed, and of the fruit of his loins—from whose loins ye are, namely my servant Joseph [meaning the Prophet Joseph Smith]—which were to continue so long as they were in the world; and as touching Abraham and his seed, out of the world they should continue; both in the world and out of the world should they continue as innumerable as the stars; or, if ye were to count the sand upon the seashore ye could not number them." Now note: "This promise is yours also [meaning you and me if we are married in the temple and live worthy of the covenants that we make there], because ye are of Abraham, and the promise was made unto Abraham; and by this law is the continuation of the works of my Father, wherein he glorifieth himself. Go ye, therefore, and do the works of Abraham; enter ye into my law and ye shall be saved." (Doctrine and Covenants 132:29-32)

It is at the altar of the temple that Moroni's promise that when Elijah came the true meaning and purpose of the gospel would be revealed to us as husbands and wives. This revelation can come in no other way. The marvel of it all, like the Atonement of Christ, is beyond our ability to comprehend. So I am of Abraham and the promise has been planted in my heart. And the Lord sent Elias and he sent Elijah. And when Elias came he brought the gospel of Abraham, not the gospel of Christ, but the gospel of Abraham, the divine commission that God gave Abraham, the marriage discipline that God gave Abraham. Elias restored celestial marriage, and Elijah came and brought the sealing power so the ordinance would be binding on earth and sealed in heaven; it takes the ministry of both of them to accomplish the purposes of the Lord. Because they came, God has planted in my heart the promise made to the fathers. And so it was that I took my bride-to-be to the temple and married her for time and all eternity, and so begins a new kingdom of God. And if we are faithful, that marriage exists here and it exists hereafter. And we receive through that ordinance every promise given to Abraham and Sarah, Isaac and Rebekah, and Jacob and Rachel. The promise is given on a conditional basis. We have to be true and faithful and keep the covenant that we make in the temple, but if we are faithful we get the blessings.

Nephi, son of Helaman, taught this doctrine to those who had newly joined the Church. "Thus we may see that the Lord is merciful unto all who will, in the sincerity of their hearts, call upon his holy name. Yea, thus we see that the gate of heaven is open unto all even to those who will believe on the name of Jesus Christ, who is the Son of God. Yea, we see that whosoever will may lay hold upon the word of God, which is quick and powerful, which shall divide asunder all the cunning and the snares and the wiles of the devil, and lead the man of Christ in a strait and narrow course across that everlasting gulf of misery which is prepared to engulf the wicked—And land their souls, yea, their immortal souls, at the right hand of God in the kingdom of heaven, to sit down with Abraham, and Isaac, and with Jacob, and with all our holy fathers, to go no more out." (Helaman 3:27-3) This is what is meant by the promises made to the fathers.

Chapter 3

The Fatherhood of God

The crowning revelation of the New Testament, the most distinctive teaching of Christ, the principle that set his followers apart from all others who professed or now profess a belief in a divine power, is the fatherhood of God. Not only did Christ profess God to be his father but our father also. We cannot profess to accept the words or teachings of Jesus and at the same time reject or seek to change or modify his declaration to this effect in any way. It matters not what sophistry is used or how cleverly it is done; to reject this, the most often repeated truth to fall from Christ's lips, that the God of heaven is both his father and our father, is to reject Christ and every other principle he taught; all that he taught was rooted in the verity that God is our father.

The Fatherhood of God

The doctrine of the fatherhood of God is the thread out of which the ministry of Christ is woven. His first recorded utterance is that of a twelve-year-old boy in the temple where anxious parents find him after he has been lost to them for three days. "And he said unto them, How is it that ye sought me? wist ye not that I must be about my Father's business?" (Luke 2:49) In the scriptural text years of silence follow until we read of him walking from Galilee to Jordan to be baptized of John. As he came up out of the waters of baptism the audible voice of God is heard saying, "This is my beloved Son, in whom I am well pleased." (Matthew 3:17)

Following his baptism he spent forty days in the wilderness being tutored by God and angels. At the conclusion of this experience came his confrontation with the adversary and the three great temptations. Two of the three temptations centered in the attempt to get him to doubt his divine Sonship. "*If*," Satan said, "thou be the Son of God" cause these stones to be made into bread or "*if* thou be the Son of God" call upon the angels to rescue you when you have jumped from the pinnacle of the temple. (Matthew 4:3, 6; Luke 4:3, 9; italics added)

To the Pharisees, offended because he made no effort to sustain their traditions, he said, "Every plant, which my heavenly Father hath not planted, shall be rooted up." (Matthew 15:13) The Gospel of John records well over a hundred instances in which Christ makes expressions to this effect:

> *The works which the Father hath given me to finish, the same works that I do, bear witness of me, that the Father hath sent me.* (John 5:36)

> *I say unto you, Moses gave you not that bread from heaven; but my Father giveth you the true bread from heaven.* (John 6:32)

> *It is written in your law, that the testimony of two men is true.*
> *I am one that bear witness of myself, and the Father that sent me beareth witness of me. (John 8:17-18)*

> *For I have not spoken of myself; but the Father which sent me, he gave me a commandment, what I should say, and what I should speak.*
> *And I know that his commandment is life everlasting: whatsoever I speak therefore, even as the Father said unto me, so I speak.* (John 12:49-50)

> *I go unto the Father; for my Father is greater than I.*
> (John 14:28)

> *If ye keep my commandments, ye shall abide in my love; even as I have kept my Father's commandments, and abide in his love.* (John 15:10)

During those sacred moments spent in Gethsemane we find the Christ praying, "And he said, Abba, Father, all things *are* possible unto thee; take away this cup from me: nevertheless not what I will, but what thou wilt." (Mark 14:36) There is perhaps no more tender text in all of holy writ. "Abba," is an Aramaic word meaning "daddy" or "papa."

Our story then takes us from Gethsemane to the Cross where the last utterance of his mortal life is, "Father, into thy hands I commend my spirit." (Luke 23:46) It is at the Garden Tomb that the first words of the resurrected Christ are spoken to Mary, "Touch me not; for I am not yet ascended to my Father: but go to my brethren, and say unto them, I ascend unto my Father, and your Father; and *to* my God, and your God." (John 20:17)

God Is the Father of Our Spirits

There is no ambiguity, no lack of plainness, no reason for confusion about what the Gospel writers are telling us. Only the refusal to allow words to mean what they say, coupled with the spirit of deceit, could result in the message being misunderstood. "All things are delivered unto me of my Father," Christ said, "and no man knoweth the Son, but the Father; neither knoweth any man the Father, save the Son, and *he* to whomsoever the Son will reveal him." (Matthew 11:27) All knowledge of the Father and for that matter all knowledge of his plan for the salvation of his children must come through the Son. "I am the way, the truth, and the life," he declared and "no man cometh unto the Father, but by me." (John 14:6)

When Christ addressed the Twelve with the question as to who he was, Peter acted as their spokesman saying, "Thou art the Christ, the Son of the living God." Christ responded saying, "Blessed are thou, Simon Bar-jona: for flesh and blood hath not revealed *it* unto thee, but my Father which is in heaven." (Matthew 16:16-17) All such knowledge must come by revelation and the revelation must come from the Father through the Son.

Thus it is that we pray to the Father in the name of the Son. Indeed, Christ taught us to address our prayers to "Our Father in heaven" because he is our Father and was known to us as such when we lived with him in heaven. "For this cause I bow my knees unto the Father of our Lord Jesus Christ," Paul declared and then added, "Of whom the whole family in heaven and earth is named." (Ephesians 3:14-15) "Furthermore," the Apostle declared, "we have had fathers of our flesh which corrected *us*, and we gave *them* reverence: shall we not much rather be in subjection unto the Father of spirits, and live?" (Hebrews 12:9)

True Followers of Christ Worship the Father

Let us turn now to the very instructive conversation that took place between Christ and the Samaritan woman at Jacob's well. The issue of the discussion was the place where the temple should have been built.

> *Jesus saith unto her, Woman, believe me, the hour cometh, when ye shall neither in this mountain, nor yet at Jerusalem, worship the Father.*
>
> *Ye worship ye know not what: we know what we worship: for salvation is of the Jews.*
>
> *But the hour cometh, and now is, when the true worshippers shall worship the Father in spirit and in truth: for the Father seeketh such to worship him.* (John 4:21-23)

As the text plainly illustrates, the Father was to be the focal point of all true worship. Christ told the Twelve that "in [his] Father's house are many mansions" and that he would go to prepare a place for them. (John 14:2) This he did through his atoning sacrifice, its purpose being to reconcile men with the Father. The word *Atonement,* which means "at-one-ment," perfectly captures the principle involved.

The Key to the Universe

It is in the doctrine of the Fatherhood of God that we unlock the meaning and purpose of all that God does. The idea that Jesus is the Son of God and that we are all the spirit sons and daughters of God is the focal point of the whole plan of salvation. From a great revelation given to Moses we learn that the "glory" of God consists in the continuation of the family unit. (Moses 1:27-39) His glory is found in the exaltation of his children. (Doctrine and Covenants 132:30-32) This is the key to the universe, the reason for its creation; it gives direction and meaning to all that God does. It was for this purpose that this earth was created, that Adam and Eve were placed on it; it was the reason their physical body was created in the image and likeness of God. It is not subject to dissolution or death and was formed of matter more fine or pure than the physical eye is able to discern. Indeed, there is no such thing as immaterial matter and all living things existed as spirits prior to their birth or creation into this mortal world in which they take upon themselves physical form. Nothing is created from nothing while the matter from which all things are created is eternal. (Doctrine and Covenants130:7-8) It is part of the divine plan that all the children of God come to earth to obtain a physical body, suffer death, and reclaim that physical body in a resurrected state.

Challenged by the Jews to declare plainly whether he was the Christ, the promised Messiah, Jesus answered saying, "I told you, and ye believed not: the works that I do in my Father's name, they bear witness of me." Understanding full well what he was saying, the Jews "took up stones" to stone him. "Jesus answered them, Many good works have I shewed you from my Father; for which of those works do ye stone me? The Jews answered him, saying, For a good work we stone thee not; but for blasphemy; and because that thou, being a man, makest thyself God." (John 10:25-33)

Here then is the great theological problem with the doctrine of the Fatherhood of God. To actually believe such a doctrine is to believe that each of us, every soul born on this earth is in very deed a child of God, having claim to divine parentage and thus being themselves of the family of gods. Jesus' long-ignored answer affirms that this is exactly what is meant. "Is it not written in your law," he said, "Ye are gods? If he had called them gods, unto whom the word of God came, and the scripture cannot be broken; Say ye of him, whom the Father hath sanctified, and sent into the world, Thou blasphemest; because I said, I am the Son of God?" (John 10:34-36)

The text Christ was quoting is found in the Psalms and was well known to those to whom he quoted it. It places God in a pre-earth assembly with his children—all of whom were then spirits—and has him addressing them saying, "Ye *are* gods; and all of you *are* children of the most High." (Psalms 82:6) If "the scripture cannot be broken," Christ declared, that is, if you profess a belief in scripture as the word of God, then you are duty bound to believe we are all the sons and daughters of God. To reject this declaration is to reject both Christ and the plain meaning of scripture.

Through this doctrine, the whole plan of salvation is opened to our view. We were born first in heavenly realms to heavenly parents and therefore the concept of family stands at the center of all that God does. By the very meaning of the word, God cannot do that which is less than godly. For him to do so would be for him to cease to be God. This would be contrary to the very idea of his existence. The key that unlocks all gospel understanding and the meaning of all gospel principles is that God, our divine Father, seeks in all that he does to enable us to become one with him; that is to become like unto him in all things. Thus salvation becomes the completion of our creation and we have claim to being saved only to the extent that we have become like him who created us.

The Plain Meaning of Scripture Lost

The fatherhood of God was the defining characteristic of New Testament Christianity. A Christian at the time of Christ or in the first generations after his ministry stood peculiar and distinctive in the world of religion because of his or her belief that God was their Father and that the meaning and purpose of every principle of the gospel grew out of that belief. The succeeding generations have witnessed a change in all of this.

The theological traditions of the great churches of the world, be they Greek, Latin, Mediaeval, or Reformed, have all found it necessary for their own purposes to abandon this principle. The adoption of the doctrine of the Holy Trinity as it traces back to Nicea in the early part of the fourth century marked an end to this doctrine and to belief in the plain meaning of scripture. This movement away from the plain and direct meaning of scripture finds its most eloquent expression in the new feminist translations of the Bible that seek to expunge from holy writ all references to God as our Father or Christ as his Son.

In a less obtrusive but equally effective assault on the message of New Testament Christianity is the removal of all references to Christ as God's "only begotten Son." The most often quoted passage in the New Testament is John 3:16, which once read, "For God so loved the world, that he gave his only begotten Son, that whosoever believeth in him should not perish, but have everlasting life," now reads, "For God so loved the world that he gave his one and only Son." (International Bible Society, *Zondervan New International Version Study Bible (Fully Revised)*, Grand Rapids, MI: Zondervan, 2000, p.1632)

The difference in translation centers around the meaning of the Greek "monogenes," which means "sole" or "only" begotten. The translators, however, have reasoned that, since they know that God could not literally be a father and thus could not literally have a son, that "monogenes" must have reference to Christ's uniqueness. So the text is twisted to conform with their theological perception. Had the word "monogenes" been used in reference to anyone else it would have been translated "only begotten."

Restoring the Light of Heaven

Our testimony to all the earth is that the clouds that have so long blocked the light of heaven have begun to part and again that light and its warmth can be felt. In the spring of 1820, a young farm boy following the injunction of James, who invited all who lack wisdom to ask of God, did so in a quiet place sheltered by a grove of trees. In response to his prayer the heavens were opened and two heavenly beings who exactly resembled each other in features and likeness clothed in the glory of heaven appeared to him. One deferred to the other saying, "Joseph, This is My Beloved Son, Hear Him!" and with those words commenced the restoration of that message declared with such plainness by Christ in the meridian day. (Pearl of Great Price, Joseph Smith History 1:17)

The event was one of profound significance. The Father once again introduced his Son, through whom it had been ordained in the councils of heaven, that all saving knowledge of God and his plan for the salvation of his children was to be had. An account of the events that followed far exceed the ambition of this work save it be said that the "key of the knowledge of God," the doctrine of his Fatherhood, was again to be communicated to all that have ears to hear and eyes to see. We confine ourselves to the citing of two declarations of that great truth that stands above all other truths—the first recorded February 16, 1832, wherein the midst of the visions of eternity Joseph Smith and Sydney Rigdon declared:

> *And now, after the many testimonies which have been given of him, this is the testimony, last of all, which we give of him: That he lives!*
>
> *For we saw him, even on the right hand of God; and we heard the voice bearing record that he is the Only Begotten of the Father—*

That by him, and through him, and of him, the worlds are and were created, and the inhabitants thereof are begotten sons and daughters unto God. (Doctrine and Covenants 76:22-24)

And again, on April 7, 1844, a few short weeks before the Prophet and his brother Hyrum Smith would be called upon to seal their testimony with their blood came this declaration:

I will go back to the beginning before the world was, to show what kind of being God is. What sort of a being was God in the beginning? Open your ears and hear, all ye ends of the earth, for I am going to prove it to you by the Bible, and to tell you the designs of God in relation to the human race, and why He interferes with the affairs of man.

God himself was once as we are now, and is an exalted man, and sits enthroned in yonder heavens! That is the great secret. If the veil were rent today, and the great God who holds this world in its orbit, and who upholds all worlds and all things by His power, was to make himself visible—I say, if you were to see him today, you would see him like a man in form—like yourselves in all the person, image, and very form as a man; for Adam was created in the very fashion, image and likeness of God, and received instruction from, and walked, talked and conversed with Him, as one man talks and communes with another. (Joseph Smith, *History of the Church, Volume VI*, Salt Lake City, UT: The Church of Jesus Christ of Latter-day Saints, Second Edition, 1950, p. 305)

Relevance to the Issue

The first article of faith for a Latter-day Saint is the declaration that we believe that God is our Eternal Father and that Jesus Christ is his Son. This declaration was intended to set us apart from the historical Christian world. It embraces the belief that God has a physical body, that he has gender, that he is a personal being, that he is an exalted glorified man. A father is a man who has sired a child. We believe we are the spirit children of God and that it is for this reason that Christ declared that we worship our Father in heaven and him only. (Doctrine and Covenants 20:19)

Thus we believe that "All human beings—male and female—are created in the image of God. Each is a beloved spirit son or daughter of heavenly parents, and, as such each has a divine nature and destiny. Gender is an essential characteristic of individual premortal, mortal, and eternal identity and purpose." ("The Family: A Proclamation to the World," Paragraph 2)

These principles, which allow us to embrace the fullness of the Bible message, stand at the very heart of the plan of salvation. "Ye *are* gods," the Psalmist declared, "and all of you *are* children of the most High." (Psalms 82:6) To Moses the Lord declared, "This is my work and my glory—to bring to pass the immortality and eternal life of man." (Moses 1:39) All of which is to say God's purpose in all that he does is to exalt his children, that is to make "them equal [with Him] in power, and in might, and in dominion." (Doctrine and Covenants 76:95)

Exaltation is obtained only in the eternal union of the man and woman as husband and wife and as father and mother. When a couple is married by the same authority by which Adam and Eve were married in Eden they obtain the promise that "they shall be gods" possessing the power of "eternal lives" meaning the power of procreation. (Doctrine and Covenants 132:20, 24) Thus salvation is a family affair and can never be separated from the union of a man and a woman. Paul stated the matter perfectly, "Neither is the man without the woman, neither the woman without the man, in the Lord." (1 Corinthians 11:11)

Be it the day of Christ's ministry or our own the most distinctive doctrine of the true follower of Christ is that God is our Father in the most literal and complete sense of the word. It is with the Latter-day Saints as it was the saints of former days—our faith rests on the word "father" meaning father, the word "son" meaning son, and the phrase "image and likeness" meaning just what it implies. The revelation announcing the restoration of the gospel to all the nations of the earth declares:

> *By these things* [the opening of the heavens commencing with the First Vision] *we know that there is a God in heaven, who is infinite and eternal, from everlasting to everlasting the same unchangeable God, the framer of heaven and earth, and all things which are in them;*
> *And that he created man, male and female, after his own image and in his own likeness, created he them;*
> *And gave unto them commandments that they should love and serve him, the only living and true God and that he should be the only being whom they should worship.* (Doctrine and Covenants 20:17-19)

In the doctrine of the fatherhood of God we as Latter-day Saints stand unique, indeed we stand alone. In doing so we do not declare ourselves brighter than others; what we do declare is that there has been a new dispensation of the gospel through a living prophet and that the key of knowledge has been turned so that the plain meaning of scripture can once again be read in plainness. Thus our testimony to all the world is that God is our Father and that he who is known to us as Jesus Christ is indeed his Only Begotten in the flesh.

Chapter 4

Eternal Marriage

Mormonism stands unique in teaching that the sacred covenant of marriage as introduced by the God of heaven was not intended for this life alone but rather for time and all eternity. The truthfulness of this declaration finds its first and most important witness in the heart of every woman who loves her husband and every man who loves his wife. Why would a man and woman who love each other want a divorce clause to be a part of their marriage covenant? Why would they want to be pronounced "husband and wife until death do ye part?" Is their anticipation that their love for one another will cease at the moment of death or shortly thereafter?

If the soul is eternal, if it is to survive death, will not the love that motivated all that the man and the woman did in this life survive also? Is it not the anticipation of humankind everywhere that their love of God is to survive death? Do we not, in like manner, suppose that our love of goodness and truth is a part of our eternal nature and that it too will survive death? If our love of God is to survive then our love for our spouse must survive also for it is the most perfect expression of our love of God and all that is right and good. What manner of heaven would it be that seeks to separate us from that which we love when it was that love that made us worthy to be there in the first place?

Does Love Cease With Death?

If death has been empowered to separate us from the love of our spouse then we must also accord to it the power to separate us from the love of our children. Of course we must ask if the heavenly ban on love stops here or reaches out to include friends and even humankind in general. What kind of heaven and gospel would this be? Might we then ask what of other divine principles? Are they too to be divorced from a place in heaven or is it only love that cannot enter there? What of kindness, charity, and the golden rule; and all other attributes that are part of the family of love, are they too to be left in the grave to return to the dust with our mortal remains? What of such principles as faith, wisdom and courage; are they, too, to find their final resting place in the grave? And if they come forth with us in the resurrection would love not come forth with them?

Such questions can be brushed aside as foolish, arguing that that love which embraces passion has no place in heaven, an argument to which we do not concede. But what if it were so; does this mean we can still love our fathers and our grandfathers, our mothers and grandmothers, our children and our children's children – just not our spouse? Having created Adam, God said it was not good for the man to be alone so he created Eve to be Adam's companion. Are we to suppose that the idea that it was not good for man to be alone applied only to Adam while he resided in Eden or that it was the expression of an eternal truth, and if eternal does it not apply in the worlds to come?

The man was created to ennoble the woman and the woman the man. Neither finds wholeness or completion alone. At issue here is whether mortality is a preparatory state for eternity, whether that which is mortal is fashioned after that which is eternal, or whether all things were created as the contradiction of what God wants things to be. Did he create Adam and Eve as male and female, two incomplete parts of one divine whole which he then joined together as husband and wife for time and eternity, "and called their name Adam" or did he create them as the ultimate contraction of the heavenly nature of things to be discarded in eternity?

"When the Savior shall appear," declares the holy word, "We shall see him as he is. We shall see that he is a man like ourselves. And that same sociality which exists among us here will exist among us there, only it will be coupled with eternal glory, which glory we do not now enjoy." (Doctrine & Covenants 130:1-2) Surely this could only be the case if marriage and the family unit were eternal also.

Did Christ Teach That There Was No Marriage in Heaven?

All Latter-day Saints with so much as a warm pulse have been told by those not of our faith that Jesus said, "In the resurrection they neither marry, nor are given in marriage." (Matthew 22:30) Thus our critics tell us that eternal marriage is not Biblical and not a part of the gospel of Jesus Christ. Properly understanding any scriptural declaration requires that we ask, "To whom is this being said?" In the application of scripture we do not want to steal promises not given to us nor would we want to lay claim to curses that had not been placed upon us.

When God said, "Be fruitful, and multiply, and replenish the earth" (Genesis 1:28), was he speaking to teenage boys or to men and women who have been properly married?

When he said, "Take no thought for the morrow" (Matthew 6:34), was he speaking to college students faced with final exams or to the newly called Apostles who were to devote their lives to declaring the gospel?

When he said, "Father, forgive them; for they know not what they do" (Luke 23:34), did he have in mind the Roman soldiers who drove the nails in his hands and feet or did he mean everyone throughout all history who seeks to crucify him afresh?

When Christ said, "Go ye into all the world, and preach the gospel" (Mark 16:15), was he giving a commission to everyone who feels so inclined or was he speaking to the Twelve whom he had already commissioned and trained?

When Christ said, "they neither marry nor are given in marriage," was he speaking to those of all generations of time or was he speaking to Sadducees who sought to ridicule him? Mark tells us he was speaking to those who "know not the scriptures, neither the power of God." (Mark 12:24-25) Luke's account tells us that he was speaking of the "children of this world" rather than those who have entitlement in the kingdom of heaven. (Luke 20:34-36)

The message seems quite plain: those who reject Christ, those who deliberately choose to misunderstand scripture, those given up to the things of the world, will neither marry nor be given in marriage in heaven. They will be as the angels or as modern revelation describes them, "ministering spirits." In so saying Christ was but echoing the doctrine taught by Malachi when he declared that those who rejected the Lord would be left with neither "root nor branch." (Malachi 4:1) These, Christ declared, "shall be cut off from among my people who are of the covenant." (3 Nephi 21:11) Such will not only remain unmarried but have no claim upon either parents or children because they rejected the covenant of marriage as administered by God to Adam and Eve in Eden, and thus the privilege is lost to them.

In the verses that precede Christ's expression on marriage we are told he was speaking to Sadducees. In the telling of the story we are immediately reminded that they did not believe in the resurrection. Like so many of our day, they had declared the Bible a sealed book placing the seal at the end of the first five books of Moses. Because resurrection is not taught in those books they refused to embrace it as part of their faith. Desiring to embarrass Christ for teaching the doctrine of the resurrection they concocted a story about a woman who was married to seven brothers and died without seed. Thus the question to which of the seven would she be married in the resurrection.

The story implies a belief among people generally that they would be married after the resurrection and that the family unit was to continue through the endless generations, hence the requirement of the law of Moses that the deceased's nearest male kin marry his widow and raise up seed to his name. The classical Old Testament illustration of this being Ruth's marriage to Boaz.

The question being addressed to Christ centered on the matter of resurrection not marriage. When Christ said, "They neither marry, nor are given in marriage," he had reference to those of the Sadducees who rejected him. His response to their question was to show that they did not understand even the limited scripture they professed a faith in. He answered their question by asking a question.

> *But as touching the resurrection of the dead, have ye not read that which was spoken unto you by God, saying, I am the God of Abraham, and the God of Isaac, and the God of Jacob? God is not the God of the dead, but of the living.* (Matthew 22:31-32)

What Christ was saying is that if their God was the God of Abraham, Isaac, and Jacob, if their God was the God of Moses, then those men must still live and if they lived their scriptures taught of life beyond the grave.

As to the eternal nature of marriage Christ had previous said, "What therefore God [not man] hath joined together, let not man put asunder." (Matthew 19:6) That is, what God joins by the power of his priesthood is to be eternal while the authority of man is limited to this earth.

The Testimony of the Bible

The authors of the Bible were a covenant people and that covenant centered in the family, a family that was to be eternal. To profess Bible religion is to profess that same covenant. The story begins with the creation of Adam and Eve and their marriage by God himself with the command to multiply and replenish the earth. The Abrahamic covenant, in which God promises Abraham and Sarah seed as countless as the sands of the sea or the stars of heaven, is but a renewal of that same covenant. (Genesis 15:5; 22:17)

The Book of Enoch describes the millennial earth saying, "And then shall all the saints give thanks, and live until they have begotten a thousand children while the period of their youth and their Sabbaths shall be completed in peace." (Enoch10:23)

(*The Book of Enoch the Prophet*, translated by Richard Laurence, L.L.D., London, UK: Kegan Paul, Trench & Co., 1883)

We testify to all who will hear it that Adam and Eve were the type and shadow of that which God desired for all his children. Every man was destined in his creation to be as Adam and every woman as Eve, each needing the other to become whole or complete. Such was the covenant that God made with our first parents on what Ezekiel calls the "holy mountain of God" and such is the covenant he seeks to make with each of us. (Ezekiel 28:13-16)

For generations it has been falsely taught that Adam and Eve sinned in Eden bringing evil upon their posterity throughout the endless durations of time. Worse still it is supposed that their sin centered in sexual transgression. No thoughtful reading of the Bible can sustain such views. It was God who created the woman and joined her to the man in marriage with the charge that they be one flesh and gave them the command to multiply and replenish the earth.

The story clearly announces them to be husband and wife before they partook of the forbidden fruit. We have it from the voice of God himself that when Eve came to Adam, offering him what we might call the fruit of life, she came as his wife and not as a mistress or a lewd woman. The symbolism could not be more perfect; it is the woman who brings to the man the fruit of life, the power of procreation, the privilege of fatherhood.

How remarkable and perfect Lehi's declaration, "Adam fell that men might be and men are that they might have joy." (2 Nephi 2:25) The statement is in itself sufficient to attest to the divine origin of the Book of Mormon. Like a mighty wind it blows away the mists of darkness surrounding the purpose of earth's creation, the necessity of what we call the Fall and thus the meaning and purpose of the Atonement.

The Three Pillars of Eternity

These three things—the creation, the Fall, and the Atonement—are the very pillars of eternity. They are the greatest events that ever have or ever will occur. Without any one of them, and without all of them inseparably woven together, there would be no salvation, no purpose in life, and no reason for being. Let us review each of these events to identify their relationship with the eternal nature of the family unit and thus a proper understanding of the ordinance of marriage.

In response to his question as to why the Lord had created the earth and how the work of creation was done, Moses was privileged to have the glory of God placed upon him so that he might be caught up into "an exceedingly high mountain" where he was shown the expanses of eternity. In vision he was shown the creation of the earth, even every particle of it and he beheld every soul who had or would dwell upon it. He was also shown other earths like unto our own and learned that they too were inhabited with sons and daughters of God.

> *And by the word of my power, have I created them, which is mine Only Begotten Son, who is full of grace and truth.*
>
> *And worlds without number have I created; and I also created them for mine own purpose; and by the Son I created them, which is mine Only Begotten.* (Moses 1:32-33)

Then Moses was given the key by which an understanding of why God created the heavens and the earth is unlocked. "For behold," the Eternal Father said, "this is my work and my glory—to bring to pass the immortality and eternal life of man." (Moses 1:39) Immortality is the inseparable union of body and spirit, it is to live forever. Eternal life is the kind of life known to exalted beings; it is to dwell in the highest degree of the celestial kingdom. With this knowledge Moses was then directed to write the story of creation that we might better understand God's plan for the salvation of his children.

The Creation

The creation story consists of three parts: first, we were born as the spirit sons and daughters of God in heavenly realms. The spirit is not some formless essence but rather is fashioned in the image and likeness of that which is temporal. This is true of all forms of life—be it the smallest spider or the tallest tree—be it plant, animal, or man himself. All things were created as spirits first; "that which is spiritual being in the likeness of that which is temporal; and that which is temporal in the likeness of that which is spiritual; the spirit of man in the likeness of his person, as also the spirit of the beast, and every other creature which God has created." (Doctrine and Covenants 77:2)

Thus all things in this pre-earth life had form and likeness, like unto that which they would know in mortality. Nothing comes from nothing—all life comes from life—all living things have parents. Every soul upon the earth was born first as a spirit to heavenly parents. The parents of our spirits are exalted, resurrected, glorified beings, having bodies of flesh and bone as did the resurrected Christ. (Luke 24:39)

Man is the prototype and pattern for all forms of life. What we say with reference to his spirit body applies also to the spirit bodies of all other forms of life. We know that the beast of the field, fowl of the heavens, and the fish of the sea, all existed first as spirits; we know they live on earth in a mortal state; we know they die when the spirit leaves their body; we know they will be resurrected and have an eternal existence with bodies of flesh and bones. We know they will be in a state of happiness and will enjoy "eternal felicity." (Doctrine and Covenants 77:2-3) That which is "eternal" is that which has been resurrected in a celestial state, which is to have the power of procreation. All life forms will thus be the eternal parents of spirit offspring, even as it is with man.

This spirit creation is followed by a physical creation. It is for this purpose that the earth was created. The spirits of all living things were now to be clothed in a tangible or physical body and to this end the earth was created. Rendering all appropriate respect to science, evolution has no place here. Men do not come from monkeys or monkeys from men; both had their existence as such before their birth into mortality, both come into this their second estate to have their pre-existing spirit clothed with a physical body. To man who was sired by a God comes the capacity to become a god; to the monkey comes the power to obtain "eternal felicity" within its own order and sphere.

Both the man and the beast are subject to death and it is in the resurrection—the inseparable union of body and spirit—that the third and final state in the story of creation finds fruition. Those coming forth in the resurrection of the just, those observant of the laws and ordinances of the gospel are entitled to a body that is now celestial, they come forth as exalted men and exalted women; whole, complete and perfect in their union together.

Herein we find "the work and glory of God" in a creation that consists of three parts—our spirit birth, our physical birth, and our birth to either immortality or immortality and eternal life. Thus God continues to expand his glory throughout the eternities in and through the family by extending the blessing of exaltation to all who choose to live a life worthy of it. (Moses 1:39; Doctrine and Covenants 132:28-32)

The Fall

The earth was created in a paradisiacal or Edenic state; one in which there was no death, decay, or corruption of any kind. Since God is not the author of such things they were not and could not be a part of the creative process. Only after all things were readied for them were Adam and Eve born. We need not mystify the story of their birth nor do we need hide behind that which has been presented allegorically or symbolically. Moses tells us that Adam "was the son of God" (Moses 6:22), Abraham refers to him as the "firstborn" (Abraham 1:3), the First

Presidency in an official statement on the matter declare him to be "the direct and lineal offspring of Deity." ("The Origin of Man") Again the record of Moses declares, "In the image of his own body, male and female, created he them." (Moses 6:9)

As my beloved friend Robert J. Matthews stated the matter, Adam was begotten as a baby with a physical body not subject to death, in a world without sin or blood; and he grew to manhood in that condition and then became mortal through his own actions. "I believe," stated Brother Mathews, "that Adam's physical body was begotten by our immortal celestial Father and an immortal celestial Mother, and thus not into a condition of mortality, a condition which would have precluded Jesus from being the Only Begotten of the Father in the flesh (Doctrine and Covenants 93:11)—*flesh* meaning *mortality.* Jesus' physical paradisiacal body was also begotten of the same celestial Father but through a mortal woman and hence into mortality." (Robert J. Matthews, *A Bible! A Bible!*, Salt Lake City, UT: Deseret Book Company, 1990, p. 188)

In their paradisiacal state God deliberately placed Adam and Eve in a position in which they had to make a choice between conflicting commandments. They had been commanded to multiply and replenish the earth. They had also been commanded not to partake of the fruit of the tree of the knowledge of good and evil. To keep either commandment required the breaking of the other. Thus it became their right and opportunity to choose whether they would enter mortality. The right of choice, that right that empowers all action, is fundamental to the plan of salvation. Had God not given to his children the power of choice and action he would have taken from them the very purpose of their creation.

Wisely and properly Adam and Eve chose to keep the greater of the two commandments, that being to have children, which, of course, required their partaking of the tree of the knowledge of good and evil. We refer to this choice as Adam's "transgression," not Adam's "sin." (Pearl of Great Price, Articles of Faith 1:3) Transgression involves the breaking of a law. Sin, on the other hand is willful disobedience. In partaking of the forbidden fruit Adam and Eve sought to keep the greater of two conflicting commandments. To do so a law was broken and they became the heirs of its consequences. The consequences of breaking this law are known to us as the Fall of Adam. With it came death, disease, suffering, evil, and all the woes of this mortal world. With it also came the promise of redemption in and through the Atonement of Christ and the implementation of the plan of salvation which makes eternal life possible.

None have taught the principles involved better than mother Eve herself, "Were it not for our transgression," she said, "we never should have had seed, and never should have known good and evil, and the joy of our redemption, and the eternal life which God giveth unto all the obedient." (Moses 5:11)

So it is, that while the world speaks with derision of Adam and Eve, we speak of them only with feelings of affection and praise. They did that which they were ordained in the councils of heaven to do and that was to bring about the Fall of man. How that event, described in scripture as the partaking of forbidden fruit, actually came about we do not know. What law or combination of laws Adam and Eve broke that they might have blood flow in their veins remains unknown to us. That they did so, however, that their brothers and sisters—then pre-earth spirits—might come to earth, gain physical bodies and prove themselves worthy of a far greater and eternal weight of glory, we do know and so testify.

The Atonement of Christ

According to the divine plan, the Atonement came in answer to the Fall. Christ came to pay the ransom for Adam's transgression. If there had been no Fall, there would have been no need for an Atonement. Thus as salvation comes because of the Atonement of Christ so it comes because of the Fall of Adam. The one cannot serve the purposes of God without the other. Existence came from God; death came by Adam; immortality and eternal life came through Christ. On this matter Lehi is the master teacher:

> *If Adam had not transgressed he would not have fallen, but he would have remained in the garden of Eden. And all things which were created must have remained in the same state in which they were after they were created; and they must have remained forever, and had no end.*
>
> *And they [Adam and Eve] would have had no children; wherefore they would have remained in a state of innocence, having no joy, for they knew no misery; doing no good for they knew no sin.*
>
> *But behold, all thing have been done in the wisdom of him who knoweth all things.*
>
> *Adam fell that men might be; and men are, that they might have joy.*
>
> *And the Messiah cometh in the fullness of time, that he may redeem the children of men from the fall.* (2 Nephi 2:22-26)

So it is that the Atonement of Christ breathes the breath of life into all things. His atoning sacrifice makes every principle of the divine plan operative. Let it then settle on every soul that seeks to know the truth that God himself married our first parents "and called their name Adam." (Moses 6:9)

"This is more than the man Adam as a son of God or the woman Eve as a daughter of the same Holy Being. Adam and Eve taken together are named Adam, and the Fall of Adam is the Fall of them both, for they are one." (Mark L. McConkie, editor, *Doctrines of the Restoration: Sermons and Writings of Bruce R. McConkie*, Salt Lake City, UT: Bookcraft, 1989, p. 202) The purpose of the Atonement is to rectify the effects of the Fall; that is to save our first parents and the union that made them one.

The earth was created so that Adam and Eve might be married. Adam and Eve fell so that they might have a family. Christ atoned so that the ordinance of marriage might be eternal so that redemption and eternal life might be enjoyed by all who have entered the new and everlasting covenant of marriage. Thus the revelation decrees:

> *In the celestial glory there are three heavens or degrees;*
>
> *And in order to obtain the highest, a man must enter into this order of the priesthood [meaning the new and everlasting covenant of marriage];*
>
> *And if he does not, he cannot obtain it.*
>
> *He may enter into the other, but that is the end of his kingdom; he cannot have an increase.* (Doctrine and Covenants 131:1-4)

Let it be clearly understood: everything in the plan of salvation centers in and around the family. It is the very work and glory of God to expand his family. To that end the earth was created, to that end Adam and Eve brought about the Fall, and to that end Christ worked out an atoning sacrifice.

The earth was created for sacred purposes—indeed, it was created as a temple of God—a place where family units are formed, the gospel taught, and the ordinances of salvation performed. God does not sit passively by when that which is holy is polluted. Consider the prophecy in the last chapter of the Old Testament:

> *For behold, the day cometh, that shall burn as an oven; and all the proud, yea, and all that do wickedly, shall be stubble: and the day that cometh shall burn them up, saith the LORD of hosts, that it shall leave them neither root nor branch.* (Malachi 4:1)

What is it of which the old prophet speaks? A promise that the wicked will be burned as stubble, but worse still they will be left without "root nor branch." It is that they will be left without family connections; family past or family future. We are told that before this happens Elijah must return, which he did, on April 3, 1836, to "turn the heart of the fathers to the children, and the heart of the children to their fathers, lest I [the Lord] come and smite the earth with a curse." (Malachi 4:5-6)

Given this perspective it is a simple matter to determine where Satan's primary efforts will be directed. Destroying the family and demeaning the institution of marriage become his chief targets. As that war that commenced in heaven continues here on earth we are again invited to stand with the Lord on a battlefield that is clearly marked.

Opposition to the Truth

Light and darkness will never meet, Christ and Satan will never shake hands. There is no middle ground where Christ and his gospel is concerned, nor is it to be supposed that Satan is now willing to surrender his objectives and abide in peace with all who disagree with him.

It must be remembered that Satan declared war on the plan of salvation long before we were born. His purpose is to destroy the family unit and he seeks to do it in any way he can. This makes the temple and the ordinances performed therein the focal point of that battle. It is to be anticipated that Satan and his legions will be found marching against the Lord's house and railing against all for which it stands for here it is that the saints of God are endowed with power from on high. That power begins with a knowledge of the truth and reaches out to embrace all the powers of godliness.

Chapter 5

Agency: "the power to act"

We have incorrectly taught the doctrine of agency long enough. The time has come to look at a dictionary, open our scriptures, and teach a better doctrine. Most Latter-day Saints have been in countless gospel discussions in which the question has been asked, "What is agency?" To which the rote answer is, "the right of choice." Check your thesaurus for either agency or choice. They are not interchangeable. They are not synonymous. No dictionary or scriptural text defines agency as "the right of choice." Under the heading *agency* my thesaurus lists such words as: "action," "causation," "conduct," "force," "power," "stewardship," and "work." Dictionaries uniformly define agency as "the power to act." *Agency* shares a common root with such words as *act, action, active, actor,* and *actual.*

In giving the gift of agency to his children God was giving a much greater gift than simply the right of choice, he gave us the power to bring those choices to fruition. It is one thing to choose strength over weakness and quite another to possess that strength. Agency is the power of action whereby the sought after strength is obtained.

The Power to Act

Let us take a story from the Book of Mormon to illustrate how the principle of agency works. Remember when Lehi and his family were traveling in the wilderness, before coming to the New World, their hunting bows lost their spring and Nephi broke his bow of steel. Without the food obtained with their bows all in their company suffered much. Laman, Lemuel, and the sons of Ishmael, began to complain against the Lord and even Lehi faltered and joined in their negative spirit. Nephi responded to their plight by making a bow and arrows from wood. He then went to his father and asked him to inquire of the Lord through the ball or miraculous director where he should go to hunt.

In recounting these events Nephi took pains to tell us that the Liahona, as it came to be known, worked only according to the faith, heed, and diligence, given to following the direction of the Lord. (1 Nephi 16:28) When Lehi sought the direction of the Lord he was soundly chastened for his complaining spirit and a sobering warning given to others of the family concerning blessings that would be lost to them if they did not repent. When they changed their spirit the direction was given for Nephi to know where he should go to hunt; which he did successfully.

The story is a type foreshadowing a future day in which Nephi, who had saved the families involved by providing needed food, would again act as the Lord's agent in providing words of eternal life for them and also for us to feast upon. I draw upon this story to illustrate the difference between the power of choice or simply desiring something and the power of action in teaching the principle of agency.

All involved in the story chose or desired, as it were, to eat. The power to act, that is, agency—the ability to provide the food, rested with Nephi. The manner in which he did so is helpful in understanding how the principle of agency works. First, Nephi used his knowledge and skill in making both a bow and arrows from the wood available to him. Then he sought direction through the channel the Lord had ordained, that is his father, who the Lord had appointed to lead them, and asked him to inquire through the miraculous director for the knowledge of where to hunt, which Lehi did. Nephi, acting on this knowledge, was able to provide the necessary food.

Lehi Defines Agency

It was the Fall of Adam that created the necessity of Christ's redemption. None have explained the principles involved better than father Lehi who said,

And the Messiah cometh in the fullness of time, that he may redeem the children of men from the fall. And because that they are redeemed from the fall they have become free forever, knowing good from evil; to act for themselves and not to be acted upon, save it be by the punishment of the law at the great and last day, according to the commandments which God hath given. (2 Nephi 2:26)

Thus we learn that both freedom of choice and agency are afforded us in and through the Atonement of Christ. Freedom, Lehi tells us, comes through our being able to distinguish between good and evil. Let it be heralded from the house tops— *freedom comes from the ability to distinguish between good and evil!*

Those who know no distinction between right and wrong can know no freedom. This has something to do with understanding what Christ meant when he told his disciples that they must know the truth for "the truth shall make you free." (John 8:32) According to Lehi, the great gift that God is giving us through the Atonement is the ability to act rather than be acted upon. Misused, this power brings "the punishment of the law" rather than the gift of freedom.

Lehi continues,

Wherefore, men are free according to the flesh; and all things are given them which are expedient unto man. And they are free to choose liberty and eternal life, through the great Mediator of all men, or to choose captivity and death, according to the captivity and power of the devil; for he seeketh that all men might be miserable like unto himself. (2 Nephi 2:27)

What we are being told here is that we obtain freedom and liberty by obedience to principles that are right and good while actions that stand opposite such a course bring captivity and death.

All choices bring their consequences, were it not so there would be no reason to make them. Good choices empower us, or as Lehi stated it, make us free while bad choices enslave or imprison us. Good choices enhance our power to act, bad choices impede our power of action. Thus right choices expand or strengthen agency while bad choices weaken or destroy it.

Agency Extends Far Beyond the Making of Choices

There are two significant reasons why we need to rise above our present tradition of teaching that agency is simply the right of choice. The first is that in the minds of many, this suggests that we have a God-given right to choose between good and evil and should we choose to do that which is evil we are only exercising the right God gave us. Nothing could be further from the truth. In all of holy writ not a single example can be found to justify the idea that it is our right to do something that is wrong. True it is that we have the capacity to do evil, no one would question that. The issue, however, is do we have the God-given right to do evil to which the resounding answer must be a thunderous "No!" The entire thrust of the gospel stands in opposition to such an idea.

President Joseph Fielding Smith stated the matter thus: "I have heard people say, and members of the Church too, 'I have a right to do as I please.' My answer is: No, you do not. You haven't any right at all to do just as you please. There is only one right that you have, and that is to … keep the commandments of Jesus Christ. He has a perfect right to tell us so. We have no right to refuse. I do not care who the man is; I do not care where he lives, or what he is—when the gospel of Jesus Christ is presented to him, he has no right to refuse to receive it. He has the privilege. He is not compelled to receive it, because our Father in heaven has given to everyone of us, in the Church and out, the gift of agency. That agency gives us the privilege to accept and be loyal to our Lord's commandments, but it has never given us the right to reject them. Every man who rejects the commandments of our Father in heaven is rebellious." (*LDS Conference Reports*, Vol. 137.1, April 1967, pp. 120-121)

In his book *Man's Search for Meaning*, Viktor E. Frankl, drawing lessons from his experience in a German death camp during World War II, observes: "No one has the right to do wrong, not even if wrong has been done to him." (*Man's Search for Meaning*, New York, NY: Washington Square Press, Inc., 1959, p. 144)

We have been stumbling over the word *right* and the phrase *civil rights* supposing that they grant freedom without responsibility. This would be like supposing that certain movements are not subject to the law of gravity. Every action has its consequence; good being restored for good and evil being the reward for evil.

The second reason we must outgrow the tradition of defining agency as simply the right of choice rather than the power to act, is that it has the effect of immobilizing people rather than empowering them. Who has not heard the parents of teenagers lament that their children are doing things they disapprove of but have no power to prevent because "after all they have their agency"? The idea here is that agency is the license to do what they want to do and no one has the right to get in their way. The idea is ridiculous. The government does not believe it. If your children, who are minors, destroy someone else's property you as parents are legally responsible. Agency does not place anyone above the law or excuse any behavior that is inappropriate. The God-given gift of agency embraces the responsibility to do what is right and can never be properly used to excuse behavior that is less than that.

To illustrate the principle, suppose you are a mission president and you have a missionary who refuses to keep mission rules. Suppose also his excuse is that he has agency and thus does not have to keep the rules. What do you do? Let him destroy his mission, or explain to him that he has the "right" to choose to be a missionary, and having made the choice, he now has but one right and that is to be the best missionary he can be; and that on any other terms you are going to send him home.

Suppose you are newly married and your husband comes home from work and says, "Honey, I met one of my old high school sweethearts at work today. We are going out to dinner together tonight. Don't wait up for me." Such behavior does not fit well with the covenant of marriage which includes the command that, "Thou shalt love thy wife with all they heart, and shalt cleave unto her and none else." (Doctrine and Covenants 42:22) Such a proposition would be offensive both to the woman involved and to the very concept of what it means to be married.

As it is in the two examples so it is in all things. No one has the right to do less than that which is right. We may have the propensity or desire to do that which is less than right but such desires are not rooted in the doctrine of agency and cannot be justified or excused by it.

Free Agents

If you have an interest in professional sports you have probably heard or read of an athlete becoming a "free agent." This means they have filled the terms of the contract they had with the team they were playing for and now are offering their services to the highest bidder or to the team that makes the offer that best suits them. Once the athlete signs a contract they are no longer a "free agent" but rather an agent for the team with whom they signed.

What is of particular importance here in our understanding of the meaning of agency is that as long as an athlete is a "free agent" no team has claim upon him or her and they cannot participate in the sport involved. It is only upon the signing of a contract that they become an "agent" for a particular team and reclaim the right to put on a uniform and participate in the sport involved. This means that an "agent" has the power to act while a "free agent" does not.

Having committed himself to a team the player accepts certain responsibilities: he has to be at practice, keep team rules, be at the games, etc. He can no longer say, "Well, I have my agency, and I don't have to do that." He has to do what he has agreed to do for which he is usually compensated very handsomely. The agent is committed to do all that he can to bring victory to his team. He cannot get on the playing field and score points for his former team just for old time sake. As an agent he is committed to a particular purpose. He can act to that end but has no right to act against it. We can change the field of endeavor but the manner in which agency functions will remain the same.

Agency and Freedom

Such a discussion raises the question as to whether agency and freedom are the same thing. Dictionaries commonly explain this as being independent, not subject to another, not restricted by covenants or laws. It is to be unattached, or exempted. Such, we have just noted, is the state of an athlete who is a "free agent." Once they join a team they are "restricted" by the terms of their contract but in the restriction obtain the power to act. In like manner, if we pledge our allegiance to a country or enter into a covenant relationship with the God of heaven we agree to the "restriction" of our actions for in that process we obtain greater freedom of action.

Thus the obedient missionary discovers that through his obedience he obtains an increased spiritual power. The husband who labors to make his marriage the best it can be obtains in the boundaries of that covenant greater happiness and blessing than he could obtain in any other way. So it is that agency and freedom while different in nature, are both enhanced by discipline, obedience and restraint.

Agency Is the Gift of God

Properly understood agency is the power to act positively. It is not a veil for irresponsibility. It is enhanced by proper use. Like the muscle properly exercised it brings with it greater strength. Every time we do something wisely and well it enhances our ability to do the same and more; conversely, to do that which is unwise restricts and impairs our capacity to do that for which we were created as the "offspring of God." (Acts 17:28-29) Agency is a personal gift from a divine Father to each of his children. Parents do not grant it to children, governments do not grant it to the governed, it is not the gift of a wise leader to his faithful followers. It comes alone from God and it is to God alone that we must account for the manner in which we use it.

You may choose to surrender your agency (which is commonly done by addiction or enslavement to practices unbecoming a child of God) but no one can take it from you. You can imprison a man and bind him in chains but you cannot rob him of the purity of his heart or his love for his wife and children. You cannot take the power of faith from him or the truths written upon his heart. There is a power and freedom even in the bondage you seek to impose upon him that you cannot conquer. You can force him to bow his head and kneel before you but through such practices you can never claim his allegiance. The Pharaoh of Egypt could imprison Jacob's son, Joseph, but he could not prevent the revelations of heaven from resting upon his captive. (Genesis 39:20-23; 40; 41:1-41)

In granting each of us the gift of agency God gave us more than the right of choice, he gave us the power to act on those choices and bring them to fruition. It has been properly argued that Christ should be the captain of our soul but even then our relationship is a covenant relationship and it is for us to advance from grace to grace as he did to gain the fullness of the power that flows from him.

Relevance to the Issue

Properly understood agency is the power to act, it is the power to correct that which is wrong, not the excuse to ignore or sustain it. No one has a God-given right to be irresponsible. As parents we cannot dismiss the misbehavior of our children with a shrug of the shoulders, a sigh, and the announcement that 'they have their agency and there is nothing we can do about it.' Quite to the contrary, our civil law holds parents responsible for the actions of their minor children. As to adults neither the laws of God or men holds guiltless those who "aid and abet" wrong doers.

As we have previously noted, no one has the right to do wrong and that certainly includes ignoring wrong doing. A bishop who winks at the sins of his ward members becomes, by that action, both responsible and accountable for those sins. At issue is if this is a principle that applies only to bishops or does it apply to parents, to all the members of the ward, and to all who claim citizenship in a nation.

The question ought to be asked as to what responsibility we have to interfere with someone else's actions if they do not believe or hold the same standards that we do? The answer is plenty! Law properly governs how people speak and dress in public whether some individual or group likes it or not. You may not believe in speed limits or stop signs but the safety of our society demands them. There are some things that a high school teacher does not have the right to teach children in class and there are some things he or she has no right to involve them in after class. Self satisfaction and appeasement is simply not a civil right and the vote of a majority does not and cannot change the effect of divinely given laws. Your community can vote against the rising of the sun but it will still rise. They may vote to negate activities that cause cancer but people will still get cancer. There is no action that anyone can participate in that does not have its consequences. Sophisticated arguments cannot change that. Agency, which is the gift of God, was given to us to make us more like God. No gospel principle has been given to us for anything less than that.

Chapter 6

God's Love

Among the teachings of Christ none gets associated with bad causes more frequently than love. It is possibly the most-often used excuse for inappropriate behavior known to humankind. Many seem to think of it as a free pass that entitles them to go anywhere they want, to do anything they want, and do it without consequences. Personal experience suggests that the loudest exponents of God's "unconditional" love are the least likely to exhibit either love or tolerance toward those who dare disagree with them.

We have all heard it said that if we would just love one another we would not need any other gospel principles. Nothing could be further from the truth. No gospel principle can stand alone; all gospel principles are very much in need of one another. Love, for instance, cannot exist without truth. Love simply cannot be the companion of a lie.

By its very nature love lifts, edifies, and builds; it does not demean, deceive, or destroy. Love does not and cannot justify sin. It can labor in patience with the sinner but it cannot embrace the sin; it cannot be used to excuse or justify sinful behavior. The parent that excuses bad behavior in their child because they love them becomes a partner with that child in the commission of their sorrowful actions. Thus both child and parent move themselves further from the light and from all other heaven-sent truths.

The Love of God and the Law of the Gospel

Foolish and tedious arguments are made to the effect that God, being God, can if he chooses save all his children. The idea was first espoused in the councils of heaven by Lucifer who, as scripture tells us, sought to destroy the agency of man. (Moses 4:1-4) If salvation consists of more than preserving men in some meaningless state; if it means making them equal with God in power, might, and dominion (Doctrine and Covenants 76:95), then salvation must embrace moral agency, which makes salvation a matter of individual choice and action and thus some will be lost. God cannot grant us agency and at the same time guarantee our salvation. For him to do so would be for him to impose salvation upon us which, plainly stated, would be to force us all to do and believe as he wanted us to. Were he to do so he could not be distinguished from the Adversary, who advocated exactly that.

There are things that God cannot do. The principle is illustrated with a boyhood experience. When in the seventh grade an antagonist of my faith challenged me with the question, "Can your God do all things?" Feeling the need to defend my God as supreme above all else I responded in the affirmative, "Certainly my God can do all things!" Then the trap, forged from my ignorance, was sprung. "Well," said my classmate who thought it his role to be the devil's advocate, "Can he make a stone so big he cannot move it?" The laugh was at my expense.

With time I came to realize that my answer to the question should have been an emphatic, 'No! Of course God cannot do all things. He cannot do anything that is ungodly. He cannot be ignorant, mean, unjust, unwise, nor can he be anything else that is contrary to the nature of godliness. He cannot lack wisdom, kindness, or justice. He cannot save someone in their sins, he cannot save them contrary to their own choice, and he cannot suspend the consequence of the laws of heaven upon those he has chosen to love.' The glory of the celestial kingdom comes only to those who choose to abide the laws of that kingdom. The grace of God makes that opportunity available to all and that same grace affirms that none will be there save it be by their choice. Anything less than that would be less than godly.

The Conditions of Love

Giving respectable names to unrespectable behavior will not change the effects of that behavior nor will redefining divine law change the effects of the law. In recent years we have witnessed the popularizing of the idea that God's love is unconditional with the appending idea that what we do really does not matter. This notion has found its way into sacrament meeting talks, testimony meetings, and our auxiliary classes. Consider for a moment what is involved here. All things that are right, good, and proper, require the existence of certain conditions for them to exist. Love is no exception. What father Lehi was telling us when he said that "it must needs be, that there is an opposition in all things," is that everything has conditions. To illustrate his point he said that if there were no such thing as "bad" there could be no such thing as "good." If there were no such thing as "sin" there could be no such thing as "righteousness." Without opposites, or we might say conditions, all things would remain, as Lehi stated it, "a compound in one."

That is to say, if God loves everyone exactly the same then love has no identifying characteristics or distinguishable effect. It would be the same as a man saying that the love that he shares with his wife he shares in like manner with all women.

While there is a form of love that a man properly ought to have that is universal and thus embraces all men, women, and children, there must also be a love that is unique and special that he shares with his wife alone. This love exists and is protected by a sacred vow or covenant that we cleave unto each other "and none else." Conditions are the life blood of this love and without those conditions it can neither live nor continue to grow.

If we lived in a world in which everything was the same color, there would be no such thing as color. So it is that if we say there is no sin we have said there is no righteousness. If the temperature is the same everywhere all the time then there can be no such thing as hot or cold. Thus it is that Lehi tells us that for something to exist it must have its conditions or its opposite. (2 Nephi 2:11-13) Repetitiously scripture tells us that Christ is God's "beloved Son." Indeed they declare him to be his "most Beloved" Son. (Mormon 5:14) If there is not some form of love that God has for his Firstborn Son, the Only Begotten in the Flesh, that exceeds the love he has for the rest of his children, these statements are both meaningless and misleading.

Scripture clearly declares that God's love, like that shared by a husband and wife, is conditioned on our behavior. On this matter there cannot be any honest room for disagreement:

> *If ye keep my commandments, [then] ye shall abide in my love; even as I have kept my Father's commandments, and abide in his love.* (John 15:10)

> *If you keep not my commandments, [then] the love of the Father shall not continue with you.* (Doctrine and Covenants 95:12)

> *If a man love me, [then] he will keep my words: and my Father will love him.* (John 14:23)

> *I love them that love me; and those that seek me ... shall find me.* (Proverbs 8:17)

> *Draw near unto me and I will draw near unto you.* (Doctrine and Covenants 88:63)

> *He that hath my commandments, and keepeth them, he it is that loveth me: and he that loveth me shall be loved of my Father, and I will love him, and will manifest myself to him.* (John 14:21)

> *And again, verily I say unto you, blessed is my servant Hyrum Smith; for I, the Lord, love him because of the integrity of his heart, and because he loveth that*

which is right before me, saith the Lord. (Doctrine and Covenants 124:15)

The great concern of those who have resisted the idea that God's love has both bounds and conditions is that they know and love someone who is not living according to gospel standards. Somehow they want the love of God to excuse the consequences of their loved one's transgressions and even in some cases prefer to find fault with the Church rather than the behavior of their loved one. Thus love gets turned into a weapon to defend harmful behavior or it becomes a bully that chases all other gospel principles out of the Church.

When you hear the refrain "How could this possibly be wrong, we love each other?" you can pretty well set it down that whatever is being talked about is wrong and those involved know it. Love is not an excuse for unbecoming behavior. What love does is lift behavior to a higher level. It is most commonly found in company with the principles of sacrifice, hard work, and self-denial. It is friend and companion to all attributes of godliness. What it does not do is go around with a chip on its shoulder picking fights with everything that does not satiate an unbridled appetite.

God's Love Is Perfect

While scripture cannot be used to justify the idea that God's love is unconditional, it does declare it to be perfect. (Moroni 8:16-17) I have had conversations with people who have argued that saying that "God's love is perfect" is not good enough and insist that it must be unconditional. Such conversations leave me wondering what it is they want to hide. The work and glory of God is to bring to pass the immortality and eternal life of man. (Moses 1:39)

We were not created for the amusement of God or for the purpose of washing windows in his heavenly palace. We were created in his image and likeness, we were created to become like him. The work and labor of God is in our behalf. All that he does is for our blessing and benefit and all that he does is infused with his love. That love holds in perfect balance the principles of justice and mercy so one does not captivate the spotlight or chase away the other. Perfect love is not going to let any of us get away with anything, but it will assure that all the righteous desires of our heart will be honored.

No Gospel Principle Can Stand Alone

Gospel principles are easily misrepresented when they are studied in isolation of each other. No gospel principle, for instance, can function independent of the love of God; yet, that love cannot supplant the purpose and place of the other principles that constitute the fullness of the gospel. All principles of truth act in harmony with each other and act for the same purpose, that purpose being our exaltation. For this reason no gospel principle can rightfully be used to condone or excuse that which is ungodly. If an expression of love is not ennobling and exalting it does not come from God. The same is true of all gospel principles; each must act in perfection and that perfection requires it to sustain and support all other gospel principles.

Consider as an illustration the placing of the man at the head of the family unit. The idea is not to keep the woman in her place but rather to keep the family unit in its place as the basic unit, not only of society, but as the basic unit of eternity. The head of the house should hold the Melchizedek Priesthood. The priesthood is named after Melchizedek because he was a great high priest whose life constituted a perfect type and shadow of Christ. The name Melchizedek consists of the union of two Hebrew words, *melch* and *zedek*. Melch means king and zedek means righteous; the name thus meaning "king of righteousness." (Hebrews 7:2)

Righteousness then constitutes the bounds of a man's authority either in the priesthood or in his home. The responsibility to see that the family is unified in living gospel principles rests with him; yet, each member of the family has equal responsibility to sustain his efforts to this end. No one, either in the Church or the family, can rightfully be called upon to sustain anything that is contrary to principles of truth and righteousness. A woman once went to Brigham Young and said, "My husband told me to go to hell." Brigham Young's response was, "Don't do it." No one has any obligation to anyone to do anything that is not right and proper.

Still there are women who are offended with the idea that a man should preside over them even though he can only do so with her consent and in righteousness. The idea simply does not bear examination. It would be no different than an argument as to what is most important to the body: the head or the heart. No body would function well without either one of them nor would it function well if it had two heads and no heart or two hearts and no head.

Equality, like all other gospel principles, does not stand alone nor can it rightfully take preeminence over other principles.

Can you imagine a doctor treating all of his patients with the same medicine so that he or she could not be accused of favoring one patient over another? Can you imagine a coach having everyone on the team play the same position at the same time to avoid inequality among the players? Can you imagine a choir director assigning half the women in the choir to sing men's parts and half of the men to sing women's parts so that both the men and the women have been treated equally?

Equality does not demand that everyone in the Church contribute the same dollar amount to sustain the Church. Tithing is a tenth whether the amount is great or small. As with tithing so with all other things, the sameness should be found in the spirit in which it is given, not in the amount.

Parenting brings with it the understanding that to treat children equally requires treating them differently. In the context of the gospel this is consistently so. The appointment of one person to lead does not demean those being led nor is it a commentary on the relative worth of those involved. We will all take our turn as leader and follower and we must learn to do both equally well. In the union of marriage equality is found only when both the man and the woman bring their best to that union.

What they bring will be entirely different and we would err in attempting to weigh, measure, or put a monetary value on those differences. The things of greatest worth are never subject to measurement, at least those measurements known to men.

What needs to be avoided is an overdose of one principle supposing it to replace the need for others. It is proper that we rejoice in the return of the prodigal but not to the extent that we suggest wayward behavior as the course to love and acceptance. When we, to protect the feelings of the bereaved family, become too effusive in our expressions of love and praise for the child who took his own life we should not be overly surprised when others of his friends seek validation in the same way.

When we open our arms to the young girl who is with child out of wedlock, we must do so in such a manner as to not suggest to her peers that what she did is the way to obtain that love and attention. Properly given, our love will shield the wayward while they gain the strength to pursue a more excellent way rather than suggest that the course they pursued represented the best of choices.

It Is Greater to Be Trusted Than Loved

As a child growing up I was confident in the love of my parents. That love was never accompanied by any idea that because of it I could get away with anything. Rather, it brought with it a strong sense of responsibility. Indeed, from my youth I was taught that it was greater to be trusted than to be loved. Thus when I read the Lord saying, "As many as I love, I rebuke and chasten: be zealous therefore, and repent" (Revelation 3:19), it made perfect sense to me.

In my young adult years I enjoyed participating in athletics. One of the lessons I quickly learned was that if the coach was not nipping at your heels, come game day you were going to see more of the bench than the playing field. If the Lord is going to use you he is going to polish and refine you in the process. Thus when I read these words addressed to the early Saints in Missouri, "Verily, thus saith the Lord unto you whom I love, and whom I love I also chasten that their sins may be forgiven, for with the chastisement I prepare a way for their deliverance in all things out of temptation and I have loved you—Wherefore, ye must needs be chastened and stand rebuked before my face" (Doctrine and Covenants 95:1-2), again it made sense to me.

God's love, as with the love of parents, brings with it the desire to do and be more. What it does not do is bring with it the idea that anything goes and that the way you live does not affect your relationship with God.

Relevance to the Issue

I am married to a lovely and beautiful woman. At the time of this writing we have been married for more than forty-five years. As in all marriages our love has been tried and tested by the storms of life. In this process the love we share has deepened and grown. It now encompasses nine children, their spouses, and a flock of grandchildren. The love that we share is both nourished and protected by the sacred covenant we made with each other and with God when we were sealed together for time and eternity in the temple. That covenant embraces the idea that we "cleave" unto each other and "none" else. (Doctrine and Covenants 42:22) To violate that covenant would seriously wound and perhaps destroy the love upon which it rests. Love is a living thing and can only continue to live if properly nourished. The same principle that gives life and meaning to our love governs in our relationship with God. Again, the key is a scared covenant. An understanding of this principle is greatly aided by an understanding of what scripture means when it speaks of our "knowing God."

Though the term is used with various shades of meaning, "to know God" in the purest scriptural sense is to have an intimate or covenant relationship with him. The Old Testament references to knowing God and to a man knowing his wife, meaning conceiving a child with her, both use the same Hebrew word (i.e., *yada*). As a man was to leave father and mother and cleave unto his wife and thus become one flesh with her, so he was to leave the things of the world and cleave unto his God and become one with him. As faithfulness in marriage was essential to the nurturing of love, so faithfulness in keeping gospel covenants was understood to be necessary in obtaining a knowledge of God. As love of spouse was strengthened in sacrifice and devotion, so the knowledge of God was obtained in living those covenants with exactness and honor. Thus a frequent characteristic of Hebrew prophecy was to describe apostasy through the metaphor of adultery, and Israel's covenant with God as a marriage. (Jeremiah 2:20-37; Ezekiel 16; Hosea 1-3)

Similarly, we read in the New Testament that Joseph did not know Mary until after the birth of Christ (Matthew 1:25), and that it is life eternal to know God and Jesus Christ his Son. (John 17:3) Both passages use the same Greek word, i.e., *ginosko*. The *Dictionary of the New Testament* defines knowledge thus:

"Knowledge was not reducible to an act of the intellect that apprehended an object. The word preserves an experiential dimension that is characteristic of it: to observe, to experience, to know, to discern, to appraise, to establish an intimate relationship between two persons, whence to choose, to elect, to enter a sexual union, finally, to recognize. In conformity with this notion of truth, to know was to encounter someone; not to know was to thrust him aside from oneself. Knowledge of God was possible because this meant a "recognition" of the one who, through his creation, was already there. To know was to be disposed to obey." (Xavier Leon-Dufour, *Dictionary of the New Testament,* New York, NY: Harper & Row, 1980, p. 259)

What needs be seen in all of this is that the modern notion of "love" that is "unconditional" is a misnomer, it is at odds with all that scripture teaches. Consider for instance this divine declaration:

> *There is a law, irrevocably decreed in heaven before the foundations of this world, upon which all blessings are predicated—*

And when we obtain any blessing from God, it is by obedience to that law upon which it is predicated. (Doctrine and Covenants 130:20-21)

All gospel laws are eternal meaning that you have an absolute assurance that they will not change. Your faith is secure. As soon as you declare God's love to be "unconditional" you lose that security. All declarations of God would be subject to change. This promise assures us that all the declarations of heaven, like the God from whom they came, will stand unchanged throughout the endless expanses of eternity. This can be so only because of the conditions that call them into existence. There are no exceptions. Were it otherwise, God would cease to be God and all the promises of the gospel would be null and void.

Every law in the universe is subject to this principle. The moment it varies whatever, it ceases to be a law and we cannot govern our behavior by it. You cannot have it any other way. To know God, to love God and to be loved and blessed of God require obedience to laws that are "irrevocable." To declare them "unconditional" is to take all meaning from them. It is to change God and to dispose of the "plan of salvation" for in such a notion there can be no plan. Such a notion—and it is a popular one—is to suppose that everyone can be saved by a God of their own making and to an everlasting kingdom of their own creation. It is in effect to say that God is made in their image rather than their having been made in his image.

This is not the God of the Latter-day Saints for with him all things are certain and all things require conditions to sustain their existence. Because of the love of God—which scripture declares to be perfect—all are accorded the same promises by obedience to the same laws; all can and will receive all blessings that they have chosen to receive. With such a God there will be no exceptions.

Chapter 7

No Unclean Thing

Entrance into the kingdom of Heaven is on God's terms and his terms alone. Were citizenship in that kingdom negotiable, could we obtain a place therein on our own terms, it would no longer be God's kingdom but ours; and would quickly replicate our present world. Thanks be to God that the terms of citizenship in his kingdom represent neither a popular vote nor the most strident voices. As the kingdom of heaven is eternal so are its laws, thus they are not subject to revision and bear no amendments.

Divine Law is the Same for One and All

We note here two singularly significant truths relative to the justice of heaven and the administration of divine law. First, the law of the gospel, meaning that which is required by God of men for their salvation, is everlastingly the same. That which was required of the man Adam and his companion Eve to work out their salvation is the same as that which will be required of the last man and woman born into this mortal sphere. The principles of salvation will not and do not vary. They are, as declared in holy writ, "the same yesterday, today, and forever." (Mormon 9:9; Hebrews 13:8)

The principles of the gospel are the same among all peoples, in all places, and at all times. There are no twilight zones in which these principles are suspended for a time and season, it matters not when we live or where we live; the laws of heaven retain their weight and measure.

The second great principle is that the blessings of heaven are dispensed according to the laws of heaven. The matter has been stated thus:

> *For all who will have a blessing at my hands shall abide the law which was appointed for that blessing, and the conditions thereof, as were instituted from before the foundation of the world.* (Doctrine and Covenants 132:5)

In like manner, the Lord has declared:

> *I, the Lord, am bound when ye do what I say; but when ye do not what I say, ye have no promise.* (Doctrine and Covenants 82:10)

The justice of heaven requires that all who are saved be saved according to the same principles. This in turn makes it incumbent upon the heavens to ensure that there will be no final judgment of any man or woman until they have had, according to God's determination, a full and complete opportunity to accept every principle of truth essential to salvation and participate in every rite, ritual, or ordinance which in like manner is necessary to entrance into the heavenly kingdom. Any theological dogma suggesting that any accountable person is to be excused from the provisions of the laws of heaven or to be called upon to stand judgment before having had full opportunity to embrace all the provisions of heavenly citizenship is inherently false and constitutes a denial of the very nature and existence of God. The argument that God is incomprehensible and thus the doctrines of heaven evidence neither justice nor mercy stands condemned by the testimony of scripture, the power of reason, and the requirements of faith which cannot be exercised in principles that are unjust and unholy.

If we cannot find within God the perfection of both justice and mercy we have no interest in exercising faith in him; we might as well join the animals and survive according to our cunning. We have it from three witnesses—the light planted in our souls at birth, the power of reason, and the testimony of holy writ—that the God of heaven possesses all the attributes of godliness in their perfection. All of holy writ rests on the divine declaration that we were created in his image and likeness and thus have within us the capacity to become like our Creator. Salvation can consist in nothing less. That which is unclean and unholy will not be called forth from the grave to form a part of his everlasting kingdom.

Ye Shall Be Holy

The final recorded appearance of Christ in the New World was to his newly called Apostles. In his concluding charge to them he said, "ye shall be judges of this people, according to the judgment which I shall give unto you, which shall be just." He then asked this question, "Therefore, what manner of men ought ye to be?" Responding to his own question he said, "Verily I say unto you, even as I am." (3 Nephi 27:27) The counterpart of this instruction as found in the Old Testament is where the Lord commanded Moses saying: "Speak unto all the congregation of the children of Israel, and say unto them, Ye shall be holy: for I the Lord your God am holy." (Leviticus 19:2) Thus the children of Israel were to be a holy people and the reason they were to be holy is because their God was holy and they were to be like him.

An ocean of ink has been spilt attempting to sidestep the plain meaning of this text. The object of such commentary is to excuse both the children of Israel, and by inference everyone else, from the responsibility to be holy. The revelations of the Restoration return us to an honest reading of the text. All of God's children are to be holy because God himself is holy. [T]each it unto your children," the Lord told Enoch, "that all men, everywhere, must repent, or they can in nowise inherit the kingdom of God, for no unclean thing can dwell there, or dwell in his presence; for, in the language of Adam, Man of Holiness is his name, and the name of his Only Begotten is the Son of Man, even Jesus Christ, a righteous Judge, who shall come in the meridian of time." (Moses 6:57)

So we have it that the Father of Adam and Eve was an exalted glorified Person, *a Man of Holiness,* and that "in the image of his own body, male and female, created he them, and blessed them, and called their name Adam." (Moses 6:9) Having thus traced the genealogy of Enoch back to Adam the inspired texts declares, "And this is the genealogy of the sons of Adam, who was the son of God, with whom God, himself, conversed." (Moses 6:22)

We turn then to the testimony of the resurrected Christ as he completes his ministry among the Nephites.

> *Behold I have given unto you my gospel, and this is the gospel which I have given unto you—that I came into the world to do the will of my Father, because my Father sent me.*
>
> *And my Father sent me that I might be lifted up upon the cross; and after that I had been lifted up upon the cross, that I might draw all men unto me, that as I have been lifted up by men even so should men be lifted up by the Father, to stand before me, to be judged of their works, whether they be good or whether they be evil—*
>
> *And for this cause have I been lifted up; therefore, according to the power of the Father I will draw all men unto me, that they may be judged according to their works. ...*
>
> *And no unclean thing can enter into his kingdom; therefore nothing entereth into his rest save it be those who have washed their garments in my blood, because of their faith, and the repentance of all their sins, and their faithfulness unto the end.*
>
> *Now this is the commandment: Repent, all ye ends of the earth, and come unto me and be baptized in my name, that ye may be sanctified by the reception of the Holy Ghost, that ye may stand spotless before me at the last day.* (3 Nephi 27:13-15, 19-20)

Thus we understand holiness to be the central theme of the book of Leviticus, and the purpose behind all the laws and rituals associated with what we have come to call the Law of Moses.

Studies in Scripture, edited by Kent P. Jackson and Robert L. Millet, states:

"Holiness can be described as the state of being set apart by righteousness. The laws recorded in Leviticus and elsewhere in the Old Testament were instrumental in training Israel to be holy. Through his system of laws, God set down rules that taught principles of cleanliness, virtue, justice, mercy, diligence, and obedience. The aim of many of the laws was to achieve and maintain *ceremonial* purity, so that the worshipers could be set apart (both literally and figuratively) from the world and found clean to enter the sanctuary, which represented the presence of God. Many aspects of laws regarding behavioral and dietary purity were symbolic of greater things and could be understood in a more sublime way by those who could see with faith. As ceremonial purity enabled one to approach with confidence the earthly representations of God's presence, purity of heart enabled one to approach the presence of God. These laws taught that no unclean thing could come into the presence of the Lord. No one who was ritually unclean could participate in the tabernacle or temple worship (representing the presence of the Lord) until he or she had undergone the requirements of ritual purification. Even something as mundane as eating provided a valuable teaching tool. Each time one ate there was a strong reminder that one was under covenant with the Lord to observe certain rules that set one apart from others. By faithfully abstaining from certain foods, and by eating in a carefully prescribed way, the Israelites had a chance to renew daily their personal commitments to their faith and the principle of holiness that it taught. In all aspects of life, observance of the Law kept Israel "in remembrance of God and their duty towards him.” (Mosiah 13:30) ...

“Calling Israel to be holy was God’s invitation to them to be like him. Ye shall be holy: for I the Lord your God *am* holy’ (Lev. 19:2). Their fathers—Abraham, Isaac, and Jacob—had all been sanctified (made holy) and entered into God’s presence. When Moses ‘sought diligently to sanctify [the Israelites] that they might behold the face of God’ (Doctrine & Covenants 84:23), they learned that it was within their capacity to do the same. ...

“To Moses the Lord said: ‘And the Lord hath avouched thee this day to be his peculiar people, as he hath promised thee, and that thou shouldest keep all his commandments; and to make thee high above all nations which he hath made, in praise, and in name, and in honour; and that thou mayest be an holy people unto the Lord thy God, as he hath spoken’ (Deut. 26:18; cf. Ex. 19:5-6). As he said elsewhere: ‘Ye shall be holy: for I the Lord your God *am* holy.’ (Lev. 19:2) Similarly the Lord told Joseph Smith: ‘Sanctify yourselves that your minds become single to God, and the days will come that you shall see him; for he will unveil his face unto you’ (Doctrine & Covenants 88:68; cf. 93:1). Within this same prophetic environment Moses came into the midst of Israel and challenged them in God’s behalf: ‘Ye shall be holy: for I the Lord your God am holy.’ (Lev. 19:2) ...

“The Lord then charged them to build a sanctuary in their midst where, said he, ‘I will meet you, to speak there unto thee. And *there I will meet with the children of Israel,* and the tabernacle shall be sanctified by my glory. And I will sanctify the tabernacle of the congregation, and the altar: I will sanctify also both Aaron and his sons, to minister to me in the priest’s office. *And I will dwell among the children of Israel, and will be their God.* And they shall know that I am the

Lord their God, that brought them forth out of the land of Egypt, *that I may dwell among them: I am the Lord their God'* (Ex. 29:42-46; cf. 25:8)." (Kent P. Jackson and Robert L. Millet, editors, *Studies in Scripture, vol. 3, The Old Testament: Genesis to 2 Samuel,* Sandy, UT: Randall Book Company, 1984, pp. 160-161, 212)

The Heavenly Kingdom and Heavenly Law

The issue here is not an isolated text the meaning of which can be debated by scholars. The issue is the entire fabric of scripture from Genesis to Revelation joined by all the revelations of the Restoration—the Book of Mormon, Doctrine and Covenants, and Pearl of Great Price. Together they declare as one voice that that which is unholy, meaning unclean, cannot enter the kingdom of heaven. Only that which complies with the law of heaven can enter the kingdom of heaven. To argue otherwise is to argue against the existence of such a kingdom. In a revelation known as the "olive leaf" given to the Prophet Joseph Smith in December of 1832, we learn that the earth itself is a living thing and thus destined to both die and be resurrected. In its resurrected and exalted state it will be of a celestial order abiding by a celestial law. The revelation explaining who may obtain entrance into his kingdom is given in this language:

And the resurrection from the dead is the redemption of the soul.

And the redemption of the soul is through him that quickeneth all things, in whose bosom it is decreed that the poor and the meek of the earth shall inherit it.

Therefore, it must needs be sanctified from all unrighteousness, that it may be prepared for the celestial glory;

For after it hath filled the measure of its creation, it shall be crowned with glory, even with the presence of God the Father;

That bodies who are of the celestial kingdom may possess it forever and ever; for, for this intent was it made and created, and for this intent are they sanctified.

And they who are not sanctified through the law which I have given unto you, even the law of Christ, must inherit another kingdom, even that of a terrestrial kingdom, or that of a telestial kingdom.

For he who is not able to abide the law of a celestial kingdom cannot abide a celestial glory.

And he who cannot abide the law of a terrestrial kingdom cannot abide a terrestrial glory.

And he who cannot abide the law of a telestial kingdom cannot abide a telestial glory; therefore he is not meet for a kingdom of glory. Therefore he must abide a kingdom which is not a kingdom of glory.

And again, verily I say unto you, the earth abideth the law of a celestial kingdom, for it filleth the measure of its creation, and transgresseth not the law—

Wherefore, it shall be sanctified; yea, notwithstanding it shall die, it shall be quickened again, and shall abide the power by which it is quickened, and the righteous shall inherit it.

For notwithstanding they die, they also shall rise again, a spiritual body.

They who are of a celestial spirit shall receive the same body which was a natural body; even ye shall receive your bodies, and your glory shall be that glory by which your bodies are quickened.

Ye who are quickened by a portion of the celestial glory shall then receive of the same, even a fullness.

And they who are quickened by a portion of the terrestrial glory shall then receive of the same, even a fullness.

And also they who are quickened by a portion of the telestial glory shall then receive of the same, even a fullness.

And they who remain shall also be quickened; nevertheless, they shall return again to their own place, to enjoy that which they are willing to receive, because they were not willing to enjoy that which they might have received. (Doctrine and Covenants 88:16-32)

Resurrection and Eternal Life

The Bible can be searched in vain for an explanation or definition of "resurrection." It is to the Book of Mormon and the revelations of the Restoration that we turn to learn that resurrection consists of the inseparable union of body and spirit. (Alma 11:45; Doctrine and Covenants 138:17) While people generally think of the world to come as one in which we continue our existence in a form like that known to us in this life, the revealed knowledge to that effect is unique and distinctive to the restored gospel.

The Bible speaks in terms of two resurrections, "they that have done good, unto the resurrection of life; and they that have done evil, unto the resurrection of damnation." (John 5:29) By the spirit of revelation Joseph Smith corrected the text to read "they who have done good, in the resurrection of the just; and they who have done evil, in the resurrection of the unjust." (Doctrine and Covenants 76:17)

All, as scripture constantly affirms, will be judged according to their works. The "good," or more correctly the "just," will be called forth in the First Resurrection. The word *just* comes from the Latin "jus" meaning law. Thus the just, or justified, are those whose course stands approved by the law, meaning the law of God. The "unjust" or those whose actions do not stand approved by the law, are consigned to come forth in the Second Resurrection or the resurrection of the "unjust."

In a marvelous revelation on the resurrection given to those of our day we are told that both the first and second resurrections are also divided into two resurrections. (Doctrine and Covenants 88:96-102) Thus in the temple and patriarchal blessings we find mention of the morning of the first resurrection. The emphasis on the "morning" implies a division of some sort which we by tradition have come to call the "afternoon" of the first resurrection. The statement in Doctrine and Covenants 45:54 describing those who "knew no law" (meaning they did not have the gospel law in this life and did not accept it when it was presented to them in the world of the spirits) "shall have part in the first resurrection; and it shall be tolerable for them," could only have reference to what we have chosen to call the afternoon of the first resurrection. We would not expect a celestial resurrection to be described as simply being "tolerable."

Those coming forth in the morning of the first resurrection will be clothed in celestial glory while those coming forth in the afternoon of the first resurrection will be of a terrestrial order. The two parts of the second resurrection will consist of those who will inherit the telestial kingdom and lastly those who will be cast out into outer darkness, thus inheriting no glory. These will be the sons of perdition.

The morning of the first resurrection will consist of three parts: first, those who lived and died between the days of Adam and the resurrection of Christ will be brought forth; the second, those who died after the resurrection of Christ to the time of his return. The third part of the first resurrection will take place following the coming of Christ in the millennial era reaching out to the end of time and embracing all who have chosen to abide a celestial law. They will not have tasted of death in the same sense that we will in that they will be changed "in a twinkling of an eye," which is to say that the separation of their spirit from their body and its inseparable reunion together will be instantaneous. The order followed in the resurrection will be from most righteous to most wicked. (Doctrine and Covenants 88:96-104)

Given that resurrection is the inseparable union of body and spirit and that it comes before we are invited to stand before the bar of God it is itself a judgment. Nephi's brother Jacob explained the doctrine in this manner:

> *And it shall come to pass that when all men shall have passed from this first death unto life, insomuch as they have become immortal* [have been resurrected]*, they must appear before the judgment-seat of the Holy One of Israel; and then cometh the judgment, and then must they be judged according to the holy judgment of God.*
> (2 Nephi 9:15)

Alma explains that death itself is a judgment. The spirits of the righteous, he said are "received into a state of happiness, which is called paradise, a state of rest, a state of peace, where they shall rest from all their troubles and from all care, and sorrow." (Alma 12:12) There is no apostasy from paradise. (Abraham 3:26) It will be with them as it is with translated beings: Satan simply has no power over them. (3 Nephi 28:38-39) By contrast, in death the "spirits of the wicked"—those who had no "part nor portion of the Spirit of the Lord" but chose "evil works rather than good"—will be "cast out into outer darkness," where there will be "weeping, and wailing, and gnashing of teeth, and this because of their own iniquity, being led captive by the will of the devil." (Alma 40:13)

In the resurrection those who are celestial will be called forth first, then will come the resurrection of those who are terrestrial, and these will be followed by those who are telestial. The order of the resurrection is from the most righteous—Christ—to the most wicked, in that order. As to standing before the judgment bar of God the degree of glory you have inherited will already be known to you and not subject to change. This experience will simply affirm the justice of God.

Those coming forth in a celestial resurrection need have no fear that in some future state the conditions of their resurrection will change. This would be like God getting sick and dying. As that cannot happen, neither can it be that those who obtained the inseparable union of a terrestrial body and a terrestrial spirit will ever be other than terrestrial or those whose resurrection consisted of the union of a telestial spirit and a telestial body. The idea is contrary to the definition of resurrection.

The thrust of all of this is that without a celestial body you cannot abide a celestial glory. In like manner, a terrestrial body is required to abide a terrestrial glory and a telestial body to abide a telestial glory, or kingdom. This principle finds expression in a variety of ways in the scriptures. The body of a mortal man is telestial in nature and thus cannot withstand the glory of a celestial being save some change is made in his body. Thus it was necessary even for Christ to be transfigured in order to stand in the presence of the Father and angels.

Christ with Peter, James, and John, were all transfigured that they might abide the presence of God and angels (Moses and Elijah) and be given the power to see the visions of eternity. (Matthew 17:1-4; Doctrine and Covenants 63:20-21) Moses experienced the same thing in his mortal ministry when he was caught up on the high mount and stood face-to-face with God. Of this experience he said, "But now mine own eyes have beheld God; but not my natural, but my spiritual eyes, for my natural eyes could not have beheld; for I should have withered and died in his presence; but his glory was upon me; and I beheld his face, for I was transfigured before him." (Moses 1:11)

Of another occasion we read: "And he [God] said *unto Moses*, Thou canst not see my face *at this time, lest mine anger be kindled against thee also, and I destroy thee, and thy people;* for there shall no man *among them* see me *at this time* and live, *for they are exceeding sinful. And no sinful man hath at any time, neither shall there be any sinful man at any time, that shall see my face and live.*" (Joseph Smith Translation Exodus 33:20) Again, the principle is that no unclean thing can enter the presence of God. It is a matter of eternal law: that which is not celestial cannot abide that which is.

Many Bible stories could be used to illustrate the point; one of the classics being when Moses came down from Sinai after having been in the presence of the Lord for 40 days. The glory that emanated from him was so great that they could not endure his presence and he had to veil his face. (Exodus 34: 29-35) Through Joseph Smith we have been told, "For no man has seen God at any time in the flesh, except quickened by the Spirit of

God. Neither can any natural man abide the presence of God, neither after the carnal mind." Those hoping for such an experience at the time were then told, "Ye are not able to abide the presence of God now, neither the ministering of angels; wherefore, continue in patience until ye are perfected." (Doctrine and Covenants 67:11-13)

The Temple

From the most ancient of days the temple has served as a symbol of the abiding place of God—the celestial kingdom. Like this sacred edifice itself, the ordinances performed therein were teaching devices to dramatize as clearly as possible what God required of his people were they to enter his presence either in this life or the next. Two psalms given in question-and-answer form illustrate the faith and purity that were expected of those seeking to enter the Lord's presence.

Psalm 15 begins with the questions, "[W]ho shall abide in thy tabernacle? who shall dwell in thy holy hill?" The answer is: "He that walketh uprightly, and worketh righteousness, and speaketh the truth in his heart. (The Book of Psalms 15:1-2) Psalm 24 contains the same pattern: "Who shall ascend into the hill of the Lord? or who shall stand in his holy place?" The answer: "He that hath clean hands, and a pure heart; who hath not lifted up his soul unto vanity, nor sworn deceitfully." (The Book of Psalms 24:3-4)

The high mountain was the scriptural symbol for the temple, representing the place where heaven and earth meet. The symbolism of the mountain assures that the path to God's presence will always be an upward climb. The holiness of the temple meant that it was a place of purity, a place where everything was expected to be perfect and whole. Elaborate preparations, for instance, were necessary to prepare the high priest to enter the Holy of Holies including several ritual washings. The procedure included his being clothed in a special robe of white linen. John explains, "the fine linen is the righteousness of saints." (Revelation 19:8)

The linen robes worn by the high priest in the sanctuary were also the dress of the angels, those who had left life in this world and lived in the immediate presence of God. Appropriately these robes became the clothing of the newly baptized. In her marvelously instructive work on the ancient temple, *The Gate of Heaven*, Margaret Barker concludes that "We must recover an understanding of this symbolism, not modernize it to a point where it says nothing, for when the meaning of these symbols is lost, the meaning of Christianity will also be lost." (*The Gate of Heaven: The History and Symbolism of the Temple of Jerusalem*, London, UK: SPCK, 1991, p. 181)

Relevance to the Issue

It is a common practice in Latter-day Saint homes for parents to remind teenage children when they go out socially to remember who they are. It would be well that we, as adults, remind ourselves also. We are members of The Church of Jesus Christ of Latter-day Saints. The name was given by revelation (Doctrine and Covenants 115:4) and was intended to be a constant reminder that all the doctrines and principles espoused by the Church must originate with Christ and that the membership of the Church are to conduct themselves as saints.

The word "saint" comes from the Latin *sancire* which means "consecrate." It was formed from the same base as the word *sacer* which means holy. (John Ayto, *Dictionary of Word Origins*, New York, NY: Arcade Publishing, Inc., 1993, p. 453) The name we bear as a Church means that we have been consecrated by the Lord for his purposes and of necessity we must be a holy people. To say that we are Latter-day Saints is to attest that those who were members of Christ's Church in former days were also called "saints." The Bible sustains this referring to members of his Church as "saints" in nearly a hundred references.

At the meeting in which the Church was organized, Joseph Smith received and dictated a revelation defining the responsibility of those who would join the Church and the blessing to which they would then have claim.

> *Wherefore, meaning the church, thou shalt give heed unto all his* [Joseph Smith's] *words and commandments which he shall give unto you as he received them, walking in all holiness before me;*
> *For his word ye shall receive, as if from mine own mouth, in all patience and faith.*
> *For by doing these things the gates of hell shall not prevail against you; yea, and the Lord God will disperse the powers of darkness from before you, and cause the heavens to shake for your good, and his name's glory.*
> (Doctrine and Covenants 21:4-6)

The idea that Latter-day Saints are to be a holy people receives emphasis in the recommend necessary to enter the temple. Many not of our faith have taken it upon themselves to criticize the Church for this practice. This can hardly be a new idea to anyone who professes a belief in or even a rudimentary knowledge of the Bible. In ancient times none but the worthy were permitted to enter the temple.

The temple was the focal point of worship for the children of Israel in both the Old and New Testaments. Following the pattern of the tabernacle in the wilderness it was divided into three parts, the outer court or court of the gentiles where all could assemble and where Jesus taught, the holy place and the holy of holies. Only a priest could enter the holy place to perform ritual there and only the high priest could enter the Holy of Holies and that only on the Day of Atonement.

The reason Moses was sent into Egypt to lead the children of Israel to Sinai was so that the Lord might sanctify them and make of them a holy nation. As they assembled in the shadows of Sinai, Moses declared the will of the Lord thus:

> *Now therefore, if ye will obey my voice indeed, and keep my covenant, then ye shall be a peculiar treasure unto me above all people: for all the earth is mine:*
>
> *And ye shall be unto me a kingdom of priests, and a holy nation. These* are *the words which thou shalt speak unto the children of Israel.* (Exodus 19:5-6)

As to the latter-day gathering of Israel the Lord said:

> *Moreover I will make a covenant of peace with them; it shall be an everlasting covenant with them: and I will place them, and multiply them, and will set my sanctuary in the midst of them for evermore.*
>
> *My tabernacle also shall be with them: yea, I will be their God, and they shall be my people.*
>
> *And the heathen shall know that I the Lord do sanctify Israel, when my sanctuary shall be in the midst of them for evermore.* (Ezekiel 37:26-28)

The principle of holiness has been lost to our society. The matter is easily demonstrated. Consider our society's loss of respect for the Sabbath as a holy day; the way the Lord's name is routinely taken in vain in the public media; and the near-universal disregard for the law of chastity.

Anciently, whenever Israel forgot who they were they forfeited the blessings of the covenant including the land the Lord had promised them. In modern revelation the Lord asks the question: "For shall the children of the kingdom pollute my holy land?" The answer to this rhetorical question is, "Verily, I say unto you, Nay." The answer, however, is limited to those who "remain steadfast ... in bearing testimony to all the world of those things which are communicated unto you." (Doctrine and Covenants 84:59-61) Those who boldly declare the message of the Restoration and stand with the Lord and his anointed declaring and defending his standards retain that blessing and promise, others do not.

Chapter 8

The Sanctifying Power of Pain

There are Latter-day Saints who have ambivalent feelings about the Church's stand on homosexuality and same-sex marriage. The issue is particularly painful when it affects someone in your own family or someone you know and love. Let us consider how this pain can be used to a positive end.

Perhaps no illustration has been used more often than that of the child touching a hot stove. Pain stands as a sentinel to warn us against danger and as a guard to prevent unnecessary harm or hurt. It can also be used as a weapon to manipulate or force people into doing what they would not otherwise do. Pain can be our servant or our master. It is for us to choose which it will be. Properly used it becomes an agent of healing. Improperly used it becomes an instrument of self-destruction.

The Family, Pain and Healing

From the gospel perspective we all come from a large family. It begins with our eternal parents and embraces family past, present, and future. An eternal family unit is formed when a man and a woman are married for time and all eternity by one holding the sealing power in the House of the Lord. The covenant made in such a marriage binds those involved to generations past and generations future. This is the reason that the heavens rejoice over us when we do that which is ordained of God and weep when we do that which is contrary to the divine order. When we do that which is right we are told that angels rejoice over us. (Doctrine and Covenants 62:3) Angels are not faceless, they are of our race; they are our kindred and as such feel our pain and our joy. Teaching this principle Joseph Smith declared, "The spirits of the just … are not far from us, and know and understand our thoughts, feelings, and motions, and are often pained therewith." (*Teachings of the Prophet Joseph Smith*, p. 326)

The very nature of our birth illustrates that it was not intended for any of us to go through life alone. We were born helpless and dependent, we live only because others have sacrificed for us. So it is that if your child suffers you suffer with them, and so with all those you love. The idea finds expression in weddings and funerals where family and friends gather together to sustain each other in times of rejoicing or mourning. It is in the nurturing power of the family that we turn to find the power of healing.

In order to understand more perfectly the principles here involved, let us commence a journey of learning together. We will follow a safe and well-marked course. We will employ the Holy Ghost as our guide, revelation both personal and institutional as our compass, and angels as our companions. We will seek protection in the robes of the priesthood and the promises of the covenants we have made. Our story will begin and end in the sealing room of the temple.

Exquisite Joy

At the time of this writing it has been but a few hours that I stood in a sealing room of the temple. Two faithful families and special friends of the bride and groom filled the room. The bride was beautiful as all brides are. She radiated joy. From the time she was a little girl she had wanted this to be the most special day of her life; and from the time her mother had first held her in her arms she too had dreamed of this moment. All present shared in her happiness. Everything about the young man bespoke the kind of person you would want to marry your own daughter. Following some brief remarks to the couple about the importance of the covenant they were about to make I invited the groom to bring his bride to the altar where they knelt across from each other. During the marriage ceremony both bride and groom wept with joy as did all present. The Spirit that filled the room was sweet and tender. Perhaps the word *sacred* would best describe the feeling in which we were all immersed.

The parents of the groom had been members of a student ward I presided over as bishop some 25 years ago. As a singles-ward bishop much of your energy is spent encouraging the young men who are of marriageable age to hold a girl's hand, and giving chastity talks. My thought as I performed that wedding was that if I had been able to bring those young people in that student ward forward in time to witness the marriage of their own children and felt the spirit associated with it, there would have been no need for the chastity talks. Then the realization came that it would not have worked, for the joy that was being experienced had been forged from the love and sacrifice that comes only in time. It required the experience that can come only in and through marriage and parenthood.

A World Turned Upside Down

All good things require their opposite. If we replay the events just recounted—in a world in which all things get turned upside down—our story becomes one in which pain replaces joy. Hurt and sorrow, which are also beyond the capacity of words to express, become the preeminent spirit. Rather than centering on the radiant bride, our story now becomes one in which a child— loved and nurtured from the moment of their birth—announces that they struggle with same-sex attraction or that they are involved in one degree or another in homosexual activities. The glory of the sun seems now to have passed behind a cloud and the warmth of its rays replaced by a biting wind that cuts to the bone.

Emotion, like blinding snow, covers everything. Hopefully the constant in our story will be the love of family and friends. In that love there is safety and in that love the strength can be found to weather this and the other storms yet to come. Yet, there can be no avoiding the fact that as in a torrential downpour everyone standing in it is going to get soaked and no amount of love can prevent it. Winter has come—gone are the blossoms, flowers, and fruits that we rejoiced in. For a time and season nothing will grow. Joy has quietly slipped away while pain boldly takes its place and with it will come lessons we would rather not have had to learn.

The Place and Purpose of Pain

Pain is a master teacher and the lessons it teaches will stick like no others. It comes in two basic shades, light and dark; the first is the power to heal, the second the power to destroy. We really do not need to be any more sophisticated than that. A side effect of a drug commonly used in cancer treatment, serves well as an illustration. It often causes neuropathy, particularly in the hands and feet. When you walk it feels like you are either walking on shards of glass or on hot coals. Struggling with the effects of this drug I went to a neurologist who told me the nerves in my feet were dead and "to just grow up and accept the fact that dead is dead." I went to a podiatrist, he asked, "Do your feet hurt?" I responded, "Yes, they hurt a great deal." He said, "Well, dead doesn't hurt."

How simple the revelation. If it is dead it does not hurt. My feet hurt and as long as they hurt there was the possibility that they could heal. If it hurts it can heal! What a marvelous lesson. Then it dawned on me, every injury I ever had hurt while it was healing. Pain and healing are the best of friends. This is true physically, emotionally, and spiritually.

Again the matter is simple, correct principles are the same wherever you find them. If you know a truth about how the gospel applies in this life you know how it applied in the pre-earth life and you know how it is going to apply in the world of departed spirits. If you know how a principle applies in the realm of spiritual things then you know how it applies in the realm of temporal things, and in the realm of emotional things. Truth is truth and it remains such wherever we find it. This means that the scriptures and the gospel are helpful regardless of the problem involved because the principles they deal with are going to be the same. In the Book of Mormon, for instance, we have a powerful story about a family deeply pained by the actions of a wayward son. The story was preserved for us because of its relevance to our day.

Alma, Pain and Suffering

In Alma 36 we have the story of Alma and his rebellion against his family, the body of the Church, and the truths of heaven. We have the story as he rendered it to his son Helaman. Alma tells how he, in company with the sons of Mosiah, went about seeking to destroy the Church and how their efforts were interrupted by an "holy angel" who spoke to them with the voice of thunder which caused the earth to tremble beneath their feet. "We all fell to the earth," Alma recalled, "for the fear of the Lord came upon us." The angel commanded Alma to "Arise," that is to stand at attention. The angel then said, "If thou wilt of thyself be destroyed, seek no more to destroy the church of God."

Alma the younger then spent three days and three nights "racked with eternal torment," which he described as "the pains of hell." His soul was racked "with inexpressible horror," so awful was his torment that he prayed that he might cease to exist both "soul and body." No such prayer can be answered and he continued to be "racked, even with the pains of a damned soul."

"And it came to pass," he said, "that as I was thus racked with torment, while I was harrowed up by the memory of my many sins, behold, I remembered also to have heard my father prophesy unto the people concerning the coming of one Jesus Christ, a Son of God, to atone for the sins of the world. Now, as my mind caught hold upon this thought, I cried within my heart: O Jesus, thou Son of God, have mercy on me, who am in the gall of bitterness, and am encircled about by the everlasting chains of death."

"And Now, behold, when I thought this," Alma recounted, "I could remember my pains no more; yea, I was harrowed up by the memory of my sins no more.

"And oh, what joy, and what marvelous light I did behold; yea, my soul was filled with joy as exceeding as was my pain! …there could be nothing so exquisite and so bitter as were my pains. Yea, and again I say unto you, my son, that on the other hand, there can be nothing so exquisite and sweet as was my joy." (Alma 36:3-21)

Building the House of Our Understanding

If we combine our temple story with the experience of Alma we can find the principles that enable us to move from a prison of darkness and indescribable pain to the realms of light and exquisite joy. To properly build the house of our understanding we must first lay the cornerstones. They are as follows:

The first cornerstone is our belief in God the Eternal Father. We believe that the word *father* means *father* and that every soul upon this earth was created in the image and likeness of God— "male and female created he them." (Genesis 1:27; Moses 6:9) We do not believe that God created his children to be merely servants or to stand in awe and wonderment at his greatness and glory throughout the endless expanses of eternity. Rather, we believe that salvation consists in our becoming like unto God. We believe that the fullness of that likeness is found only in the family unit. Salvation is a family affair.

The second cornerstone is our belief that Jesus the Christ is in very deed the Son of God. We believe that in and through his atoning sacrifice all the spirit offspring of God who choose to comply with the laws and ordinances of the gospel may be saved—meaning exalted in the highest of the heavenly kingdoms. The purpose of the Atonement being to reconcile us with the Father, that is, to free us from the affects of Adam's Fall and from the effects of our own transgressions that we might become fit citizens of a heavenly kingdom.

The third cornerstone is our belief in the Holy Ghost as the third personage in the godhead. The roles of the Holy Ghost embrace that of Comforter, Sanctifier, Revelator and Witness. As a Comforter, he brings to the heart and soul of man the assurance of heaven that we are pursuing a course pleasing to God and that all is well. As a Sanctifier, the Holy Ghost purges our soul of all that is unclean and impure that we might receive revelation and entertain angels. As a Revelator, he is the medium through which the mind and will of the Lord is granted to us. As a Witness, he confirms all heaven-sent truths in a manner that excels and exceeds any other.

The fourth cornerstone is our belief in the power and authority of the priesthood. We believe that the priesthood "administereth the gospel," and that it is through the higher or holy priesthood that the blessings of the Atonement are ministered. (Doctrine and Covenants 84:19) Each ordinance of salvation being in and of itself a 'key word,' meaning that in and through each ordinance knowledge and understanding that could not otherwise be had is unlocked or revealed to us.

Having laid these cornerstones we can now build the house of our understanding. In doing so, we will use the pattern and design of the Lord's house. In all gospel dispensations the Lord has directed his people to build temples where he might "endow" them "with power" from on high. Thus we seek to fashion our faith after that pattern. The word "endow" means "to clothe" or to "put on power." The scriptural promises granted to those who have been endowed include being "taught from on high," being "filled with light," entertaining angels, and being blessed with the capacity to comprehend all things. (Doctrine and Covenants 43:16; Luke 24:49; 84:88; 88:67)

The endowment must be preceded by the ordinance of baptism which brings with it the gift or companionship of the Holy Ghost. "No man," the Prophet Joseph Smith taught, "can receive the Holy Ghost without receiving revelations." (*Teachings of the Prophet Joseph Smith*, p. 328) It is not of a single revelation of which we speak, but a continuing series of revelations. The pattern being "line upon line, precept upon precept, here a little and there a little." (2 Nephi 28:30) And so it is that we proceed in confidence and faith knowing that as direction is needed it will come.

The Ministry of Angels

Let us now return to the matter of the ministering of angels. In doing so let it be remembered that we have but one gospel and its principles apply to all in the same manner. Thus we know if angels administered to people anciently then they must administer in like manner to people today. If it is not so then the gospel is not so. If angels came in Bible or Book of Mormon times to aid parents in protecting, directing, and correcting their children they must come in like manner today. It is not required that they speak with thunder nor is it required that they cause the ground to quake. But that they come and that they get the attention of those to whom they come is as much a part of the gospel as baptism, the sacrament, and long meetings.

If the family unit is not eternal, if family councils are not held on the other side of the veil, if assignments are not made to look after their kin in the flesh, if their hearts are not pained by our actions as the Prophet said, and if angels, as Paul declared, have not "entertained" many "unawares," then forget it; the gospel is just a security blanket for the simple-minded. On the other hand, if God lives then there are angels who administered to his Son, and if the laws of heaven are immutable, they can administer to my sons and my daughters and your sons and your daughters.

If you believe the Book of Mormon you have to believe this. The story of the Book of Mormon is the story of Moroni coming back with a message for his children. That's the principle of which we speak. The same principle holds for the Bible-believing world. In the Book of Malachi (which should have been translated the Book of Angels because that is what the word *Malachi* means) we are told that Elijah the prophet is to come and turn the heart of the fathers to the children and the heart of the children to the fathers and that if this does not happen there was no purpose in creating the earth in the first place. (Malachi

4:5-6) Well, Elijah came and because he came the right rests with our righteous fathers on the other side of the veil to come and minister to wayward children today just as they did in Alma's day.

If there is a God, a prophet named Elijah, and the word of the Bible is to be believed, then our pain is shared by our families on the other side of the veil and they have been granted power beyond that which we have to do something about it.

The Power of the Priesthood

As to the matter of the priesthood, we have already observed that the Lord said that the higher "priesthood administereth the gospel." (Doctrine and Covenants 84:19) The full text reads as follows:

> *And this greater priesthood administereth the gospel and holdeth the key of the mysteries of the kingdom, even the key of the knowledge of God.*
>
> *Therefore, in the ordinances thereof, the power of godliness is manifest.*
>
> *And without the ordinances thereof, and the authority of the priesthood, the power of godliness is not manifest unto men in the flesh;*
>
> *For without this no man can see the face of God, even the Father, and live.* (Doctrine and Covenants 84:19-22)

The Lord's house is a house of order. The gospel does not run rampant nor is it a smorgasbord from which we pick and choose that which we will embrace and that which we will not. The priesthood is the authority by which the gospel is governed and all its blessings administered. It embraces the power to heal, and to sanctify. We must draw upon these blessings if we are to succeed. We, like Abraham of old, must seek after the blessings of heaven. We must make fasting, prayer, priesthood blessings, the administration of angels, and all the blessings of the endowment real. "For what doth it profit a man if a gift is bestowed upon him, and he receive not the gift? Behold, he rejoices not in that which is given unto him, neither rejoices in him who is the giver of the gift." (Doctrine and Covenants 88:33)

Resolving Pain

Having built the house of our understanding, the house of our faith, we can take refuge therein. Thus it is to home and family that we turn to heal pain. We now do so with the understanding that any effort to escape the pain of which we speak, save it is done in accord with the system instituted by the Lord himself, will fail. We can join our errant child, we can immerse them in all the love to be found in this and all other universes combined and it will not be enough. Love is an integral part of the gospel but it is not the gospel. Love ceases to be what we suppose it to be when we divorce it from the companionship of other gospel principles and let it become something of a tyrant holding all other principles hostage.

When love is coupled with faith and obedience it becomes a life-giving force. When it is used simply to excuse us from personal responsibility and from the need for obedience to all the laws and ordinances of the gospel, like the field bindweed (some call morning glory) in our gardens, it reaches out and strangles everything that competes with it for space.

In so saying, we are completely aware there are those not of our faith who will greet such a statement with anger, telling us that such things as temples, ordinances, priesthood, and repentance were all done away with in the Atonement of Christ. They would have us suppose that it is for everyone to read the Bible, accept Christ and then make a self determination as to what constitutes salvation on their part. To which we respond that if the conditions for entrance into our Heavenly Father's kingdom are not of his making then the kingdom is not of his making either. If they do not represent principles that are eternal then in like manner the kingdom cannot be eternal.

What then is the grand key? *No course of action can succeed in bringing the necessary healing save it leads to the temple. All that we do must be measured by this standard: "Does it lead to the temple?"*

The Necessary Help

Building on that foundation, let us become more mundane—while you have your eyes to the heavens you must keep your feet on the ground. To that end we make these suggestions:

>   1.   Those inflicted by the pain associated with same-sex attraction must counsel with their appropriate ecclesiastical leader. Normally this will be a bishop. Certainly this means the person involved but it also may include parents, siblings, or close friends. If you got soaked in the torrent of emotion, dry out in the bishop's office.
>
>   2.   As appropriate, seek professional counseling. Do so under the direction of your bishop or ecclesiastical leader. Be aware that the Church has designed programs to help here. Remember that all counselors are not created equal.
>
>   3.   Be extremely careful about your circle of friends. If you pal with people who love darkness rather than light then that is where you will find yourself. If your companions are people who are temple-worthy then that is where you are going to find yourself.
>
>   4.   Choose carefully the voices you listen to. No truth that matters goes unopposed. The greater a truth is the greater the heresy that will stand opposite it. The Devil will appoint the most eloquent of his disciples to address the most damning issues. The truth stands on its own. The Lord clothes his servants in the robes of righteousness. The Devil clothes his servants in

whatever eloquence is necessary to hide what is really being said. Listen to those you wish to be like.

5.   Parents, family and friends, let it be known that you are there to love and support—most of which you must do silently. Do not become the problem trying to solve the problem.

6.   Seek the blessings of the priesthood. Some months ago my wife accepted an invitation for me to give a blessing to a very troubled young man. I knew his history too well and wanted no part of it. Just the same I kept the appointment and gave the blessing and learned one of the important lessons of my life. Judgment does not rest with me. The God of heaven had a remarkable blessing and promise for the young man and invited me to deliver it because of what I would learn in the process. Add to the blessing of the priesthood the administration of angels as already discussed. These things are real.

7.   Never give up. Know that God will not.

Conclusion

Pain and suffering are a part of the healing process. (Alma 42:16-18) In teaching this principle Elder Dallin H. Oaks asked, "Why is it necessary for us to suffer on the way to repentance for serious transgressions? We often think of the results of repentance as simply cleansing us from sin. But that is an incomplete view of the matter. A person who sins is like a tree that bends easily in the wind. On a windy and rainy day the tree bends so deeply against the ground that the leaves become soiled with mud, like sin. If we only focus on cleaning the leaves, the weakness in the tree that allowed it to bend and soil its leaves may remain. Merely cleaning the leaves does not strengthen the tree. Similarly, a person who is merely sorry to be soiled by sin will sin again in the next high wind. The susceptibility to repetition continues until the tree has been strengthened." ("Sin and Suffering," an address given at Brigham Young University, August 5, 1990)

Thus pain becomes the agent of sanctification; its purpose is to heal, and to make clean. It brings a strength that can be obtained in no other way. To heal, pain must be coupled with love—love, like pain, comes in different shades. Clothed in purity it edifies and strengthens; it finds its expression in joy. In its darker forms it seeks only to excuse, justify, and alienate you from the covenants you have with God and family both past, present, and future. It leads to the temple of darkness not the temple of the Lord. It eschews the idea of priesthood and thus rejects that power by which the blessings of the Atonement are administered.

Thus we chart our longitude and latitude by asking a simple question, "Does the course we are following lead to the sealing room of the temple?"

Chapter 9

What Would Jesus Do?

A crucial issue facing our nation at the present time centers in the definition of marriage. Should it be expanded to embrace same-sex couples; that is, should a man be allowed to marry another man or a woman another woman? Many have taken up the fight, proclaiming this to be the last frontier of civil rights. Others wonder if this parade wandered down the wrong street and if the issue has anything at all to do with civil rights.

As Latter-day Saints our faith embraces the belief that the Constitution of the United States is divinely inspired. We believe it was instrumental in giving birth to our nation and that the principles found therein are fundamental to the preservation of this nation. We believe its divine purpose embraces the protection of the "rights" of "all flesh," according to "just and holy principles." (Doctrine and Covenants 101:77) That is to say, we believe the Constitution was written to protect the natural rights of everyone within its reach in their pursuit of that which is just and holy.

We believe that to be "just" a principle must first be "holy." It cannot be rooted in any other soil. True justice represents the application of eternal truths. It is thus a lion in the path of all who argue against divinely revealed truths seeking to ban them from our schools and public discussion. If it has been revealed to us that we are the children of God, created in his image and likeness, then that knowledge must be foundational to all that we do in both the private and public arena. The scales of justice must always be in balance with that which is holy. It is through the lens of eternal truth that we must view the destiny of our nation and the principles that govern it. For us to argue from other principles is for the blind to lead the blind and for both to fall into the ditch. (Matthew 15:14)

We reject the idea that our nation's Constitution was written to protect as a right the efforts of some to destroy it or the efforts of others to use it as a shield to justify that which is neither right nor holy. That is to say, no one has a lawful right to do that which is wrong.

Our faith embraces the belief that we are all born into this life with the light of Christ planted in our hearts and that we will be led to do what is right if we so choose. (Moroni 7:16; Doctrine and Covenants 84:45-48; 93:1-2)

We believe that we share the responsibility that rests upon every citizen of this land to do that which is in our power to sustain the Constitution according to the best light the God of heaven has seen fit to bestow upon us. It is to that end that that which follows has been written. My purpose is simply to set forth correct principles in clarity and plainness.

As Latter-day Saints we believe that marriage was ordained of God; that this sacred union of man and woman has been entrusted by God with the power to give life and the attendant responsibility to nurture and protect that life. The family unit thus created becomes the primary source for teaching virtues that constitute the foundation of society for both this world and the next.

The Just and the Holy

In 1833, mobs drove the early Saints of this dispensation from their homes and farms in Jackson County, Missouri. They were instructed by the Lord to seek redress—

> *According to the laws and constitution of the people, which I [God] have suffered to be established, and should be maintained for the rights and protection of all flesh, according to just and holy principles; That every man may act in doctrine and principle pertaining to futurity, according to the moral agency which I have*

given unto him, that every man may be accountable for his own sins in the day of judgment. Therefore, it is not right that any man should be in bondage one to another. And for this purpose have I established the Constitution of this land, by the hands of wise men whom I raised up unto this very purpose, and redeemed the land by the shedding of blood. (Doctrine and Covenants 101:77-80)

To more fully understand the meaning of the words "just" and "holy" as used in this revelation, we turn to Noah Webster's 1828 dictionary. Here we learn that that which is just is that which "conforms to the law," that which is "righteous" or "upright." In its etymology the word "just" traces back to that which was "ritually pure." That which is just is that which conforms "exactly to the laws, and to principles of rectitude in social conduct."

The word "holy" was understood to be that which is "whole" and thus "in the image of God." It is that which was "free from sin and sinful affections." (Noah Webster, *Noah Webster's First Edition of an American Dictionary of the English Language* [1828], facsimile edition, Anaheim, CA: Foundation for American Christian Education, 1967) It is the purpose of this work to present with plainness and clarity holy principles as they are taught in scripture relative to the institution of marriage. That is, to defend the traditional institution by the light of the Restored gospel. In doing so, I assume responsibility for that which I have written just as the reader must assume responsibility for that which they choose to believe and the causes they choose to support.

Inalienable and Civil Rights

Inalienable or natural rights are ours by birth. They are the gift of God and no one has the right to take them from us. As our guiding text announces, "it is not right that any man should be in bondage one to another." It is also fundamental to our understanding that all rights given us by God represent a covenant relationship with him and that we are accountable to him for how we use them. No right exists without responsibility; responsibility that embraces both God and all humankind. Again, our guiding text states the matter thus: "every man may act in doctrine and principle pertaining to futurity, according to the moral agency which I have given unto him, that every man may be accountable for his own sins in the day of judgment." (Doctrine and Covenants 101:77-80)

The formation of a state or nation requires the surrender of lawless or wanton behavior on the part of all who desire the protection and blessings that come with citizenship. You agree to respect my property and I agree to respect yours. We agree to pay taxes so that we and our families can enjoy such things as roads, police and fire protection and the general freedom of commerce.

The government in turn agrees to protect and defend certain of our rights both from its own infringement and that of others. We refer to these rights of citizenship as civil rights. We recognize the right to marry as a civil right. Indeed, a marriage is a contract between two people and the state in which it is performed.

I am a temple sealer and as such have the authority to marry a man and woman for time and for all eternity. The sealing power with which I have been entrusted traces directly to the Prophet who stands at the head of the Church and Kingdom of God on earth and through him, in a few short steps, to the Lord Jesus Christ. Strict discipline attends the use of this authority and should I fail to adhere to that discipline, this sacred trust would quickly be lost to me.

Sacred ordinances must be performed with exactness; it is not within my purview to either add to or take from the marriage ritual as it has been revealed. Anything I might choose to say by way of encouragement, counsel, or instruction to the couple being married must be worthy of the temple; and it must accord naturally and appropriately with the sacred covenant those being married are making. It is required that the couple be clothed in the robes of righteousness and to kneel at the altar of the temple to be married. Those robes symbolize the virtue, cleanliness, and obedience that constitute the most important part of the preparation they have made to enter into this sacred covenant. The same standard of righteousness is required of all who are in attendance at the marriage, including myself as the sealer.

Of significance is the fact that I cannot enter the sealing room to perform the ordinance of marriage without the authorization of the state, nor can the couple desiring to be married come to the temple for that purpose save they bring with them a valid marriage license which only the state can issue. The principle is universal: as a chaplain in the military I performed marriages by the authority of the Army of the United States; as a mission president in Scotland I performed a marriage by the authority of the Queen of England; as a bishop I performed marriages by the authority of the state.

To act lawfully in each instance I acted with the permission and under the direction of the authority mentioned. It is foundational to the existence of the state that it holds authority over the institution of marriage. In the legal sense marriage is a three-cornered contract, made between the persons who wish to marry and the state in which the marriage takes place. In the spiritual sense the marriage is a sacred covenant between the persons being married and God; on this matter the state remains silent.

The state holds its authority over the marriage union very jealously. No legal or lawful marriage can be performed in any state of the union without the consent of the state. While the state may choose to delegate the authority to perform the marriage to others, it holds without compromise the right to determine who can be married and under what circumstances a divorce or the dissolution of the marriage can take place.

The fact that all states retain control over the institution of marriage constitutes the irrefutable evidence that marriage and the family are fundamental to the survival of the social fabric of society and the very existence of the state itself. Marriage exists as much for society as it does for the couple. The fact that all churches that form a part of the society assent to the states' role in controlling the institution of marriage is the irrefutable proof that the God of the American people sustains the role of the state in so doing. That is to say, God would have it so.

Every ennobling characteristic known to humankind finds its greatest exponent in the family. Without the influence of good families no society can survive. To that end no state or nation has any greater duty than to look after and protect the well-being of the family unit. There is no action that weakens the family unit that does not at the same time weaken the nation of which that family is a part.

What Would Jesus Do?

The question "What would Jesus do?" is often imposed on the discussion relative to whether the traditional definition of marriage should be redefined to include same-sex marriages. The response given to this question is determined by *which* Jesus those answering have chosen to follow. In a prophetic description of the last days Christ said, "Many shall come in my name, saying, I am Christ; and shall deceive many." (Matthew 24:5) As prophesied, the deceptions have been plentiful.

Virtually every social movement claims that Christ is marching with them. A distinctively curious thing about this is that the Jesus of the New Testament never associated himself with such movements though he had more than ample opportunity to do so. He did not seek to change the laws of men but rather sought to change the hearts of men. He did not seek to mandate salvation by legislation.

The three most distinctive characteristics of the "Jesus" associated with the same-sex marriage movement are his love and approval of all who sustain their cause; his obvious disdain for those who oppose it; and his willingness to ignore the profane manner in which his name and doctrines are treated by his newly found disciples.

What we are being asked to do here is to suppose that since the time of his mortal ministry Christ has changed his mind on pretty much everything that he taught in New Testament times. It would appear that given the chance to do things over again he would want to be more open, more loving, more forgiving, and more tolerant. Apparently, he now feels that during his mortal ministry he was too harsh and divisive. Perhaps he has reassessed teachings that attracted only a small group of people and resulted in their having to flee their homes and hide in the wilderness.

So the question is, has the time come for us to rewrite, redefine, and reinterpret what Christ did and said in light of wisdom unknown to his day? Is it not our obligation to liberate those about us from the traditions of their fathers, having discovered that their fathers who had the power to call down the blessings of heaven were in bondage to false traditions?

If, on the other hand, we are to answer the question as to what would Christ do by a thoughtful consideration of what he did during his mortal ministry—assuming the principles to be applicable to those of all ages—then our answer is that:

He would conform in all things to the will of his Father, neither adding to nor taking from any gospel ordinance or principle; but teach all things as instituted from before the foundation of the earth.

He would follow a path of virtue and holiness teaching others to do the same. Without compromise he would teach the doctrine of repentance and that no unclean thing can enter into the presence of God.

He would give his life as a ransom for the sins of all who would repent, making it possible for them to return to the presence of their eternal Father.

What then would Jesus do? He would do precisely what he has done. He would inspire people of faith and virtue to flee the suppressing captivity of the Old World and come to the New World where they could worship according to the dictates of their conscience. Here he would deliver them out of the hands of all other nations in a great Revolutionary War and inspire them in forming a government that would preserve religious freedom to all its citizens.

He would then restore anew among them the fullness of his everlasting gospel centering in the calling of a living prophet, the restoration of the priesthood, and the restoration of the new and everlasting covenant, all according to the promises given to Israel anciently.

What then would Jesus do? He would have his people—those who had gathered from the ends of the earth, those who had come to America as husbands and wives and as fathers and mothers—build a temple to his name where they could kneel at the altar and be sealed as families for time and for all eternity. This was the very reason for the restoration of the gospel and the formation of this nation and the promises given to their fathers anciently. He would then have them take this message of salvation to all the nations of the earth and build temples among all the peoples of the earth so that those of every nation, kindred, tongue, and people might be united together in family units that are eternal.

Relevance to the Issue

We believe this nation was created by the hand of God for a divine purpose. A battle now rages among its citizenry, over the issue of same-sex marriage, those advocating this cause do so under the banner of justice, liberty, and civil rights. Those opposed to this "new morality" wonder how such a discussion ever got cast in such terms. The marriage issue, however, is but a battle in a greater war, the sexual revolution which demands not simply tolerance of behavior once thought reprehensible, but acceptance, honor, with special status being accorded to them by law.

This new religion, and religion it is, has chosen our courts of law and halls of Congress as their sanctuaries and temples. Here in their system of worship they seek to clothe themselves in a freedom of expression which they in turn unflinchingly deny to others. You cannot redefine the family without redefining the curriculum of our public schools, dictating the doctrine and practices of our churches, and shackling the freedom of expression now enjoyed in the press, on television, and radio.

Let us state the matter plainly; the traditional family is founded on a moral covenant. Everything associated with the current sexual revolution is at war with that covenant. Our defense must rest on the declaration of our faith in God, our covenant with him, and the clear recognition of right and wrong. To seek victory on any other terms—than our faith in God and the principles revealed through him—is to concede defeat. Doing the right thing for the wrong reason is never the right thing. It is to build a castle out of sand in the hope that the tide will not come in.

Well might we remind ourselves that it was in the command that they honor father and mother that ancient Israel received the promise that their days would be long upon the land which the Lord had given to them. Are we now to suppose that this principle no longer applies? Can we now in the days of our "enlightenment" disregard the role of father and mother and expect that our nation will long survive?

There are those who have chosen not to stand and be counted, reasoning that Christ is about to return and bring an end to all that is inappropriate. In so reasoning they have put their children and their children's children in great peril. If salvation consists in being Christ-like, perhaps we ought to be found doing the kind of things we expect him to do.

Sources

Ayto, John, *Dictionary of Word Origins*, New York, NY: Arcade Publishing, Inc., 1993

Ayto, John, *Word Origins*, London, UK: A & C Black, 2008

Barker, Margaret, *The Gate of Heaven: The History and Symbolism of the Temple of Jerusalem*, London, UK: SPCK, 1991

Beck, Julie B., "Teaching the Doctrine of the Family," an address given at the LDS Conference Center in Salt Lake City, August 4, 2009, www.lds.org/pa/rs/pdf/CES_2009_Beck_eng.pdf

Berlin, Adele and Brettler, Marc Zvi, editors; Fishbane, Michael, consulting editor, *The Jewish Study Bible*, New York, NY: Oxford University Press, 2004

Cannon, George Q., editor, *Journal of Discourses, Vol. 9*, Liverpool, UK: Cannon, 1862

The First Presidency and Council of the Twelve Apostles of the Church of Jesus Christ of Latter-day Saints, "The Family: A Proclamation to the World," September 23, 1995; *Ensign*, November 1995

The First Presidency of the Church of Jesus Christ of Latter-day Saints (Joseph F. Smith, John R. Winder, Anthon H. Lund), "The Origin of Man," *Improvement Era*, November 1909 [notation standardized]

Frankl, Viktor, *Man's Search for Meaning*, New York, NY: Washington Square Press, Inc., 1959

Hunter, Howard W., "A Temple-Motivated People," *Ensign*, February 1995

International Bible Society, *Zondervan New International Version Study Bible (Fully Revised)*, Grand Rapids, MI: Zondervan, 2000

Jackson, Kent P. and Millet, Robert L., editors, *Studies in Scripture, vol. 3, The Old Testament: Genesis to 2 Samuel*, Sandy, UT: Randall Book Company, 1984

Laurence, Richard, L.L.D. (translated by), *The Book of Enoch the Prophet*, London, UK: Kegan Paul, Trench & Co., 1883

LDS Conference Reports, Vol. 137.1, April 1967

Leon-Dufour, Xavier, *Dictionary of the New Testament*, New York, NY: Harper & Row, 1980

Matthews, Robert J., *A Bible! A Bible!*, Salt Lake City, UT: Deseret Book Company, 1990

McConkie, Bruce R. (compiled by), *Doctrines of Salvation: Sermons and Writings of Joseph Fielding Smith, Vol. 1*, Salt Lake City, UT: Bookcraft, 1954

McConkie, Mark L., editor, *Doctrines of the Restoration: Sermons and Writings of Bruce R. McConkie*, Salt Lake City, UT: Bookcraft, 1989

Oaks, Dallin H., "Sin and Suffering," an address given at Brigham Young University, August 5, 1990, http://speeches.byu.edu/?act=viewitem&id=567

Richards, Franklin D. and Little, James A., *A Compendium of the Doctrines of the Gospel*, Salt Lake City, UT: Deseret Book Company, 1925

Shipley, Joseph T., *Dictionary of Word Origins*, New York, NY: Philosophical Library, 1945

Smith, Joseph, *History of the Church, Volume VI*, Salt Lake City, UT: The Church of Jesus Christ of Latter-day Saints, Second Edition, 1950

Smith, Joseph Fielding (compiled by), *Teachings of the Prophet Joseph Smith*, Salt Lake City, UT: Deseret Book Company, 1976

Talmage, James E., "The Eternity of Sex," *Young Woman's Journal*, October 1914

Webster, Noah, *Noah Webster's First Edition of an American Dictionary of the English Language* [1828], facsimile edition, Anaheim, CA: Foundation for American Christian Education, 1967

- - - - - - - - - - - - - - - -

The scriptures cited herein are from the four "standard works" of The Church of Jesus Christ of Latter-day Saints:

The Holy Bible, Authorized King James Version, Containing the
    Old and New Testaments (published 1979)
The Book of Mormon: Another Testament of Jesus Christ (1981)
    The Doctrine and Covenants (1981)
    The Pearl of Great Price (1981)

Also referenced is the Bible Dictionary (1979)